"PORTRAITS & CARICATURES OF YESTERDAY'S POLITICAL MEN"

Drawn by JOHN CALVERT

Foreword by Robin Calvert

FOREWORD

My father, born October 7 1921, in Knaresborough, North Yorkshire, came from a large family.

His father saw action in many WW1 trouble spots, including the Somme and Passchendaele. He was badly gassed, dying in 1940.

My father joined rather than conscripted into the Army and spent many hours on the searchlights, billeted – as all soldiers were – around the country, including Scotland (the Black Watch Regiment), Lincolnshire and Wiltshire.

My father was self-employed and then worked as a carpenter. Yet in retirement he liked nothing better than to sit down and write poetry (published by Anchor Books & SKP Books in the 1990s), or draw likenesses –

usually from photographs, occasionally cartoons - of well-known figures from the world of showbusiness and politics.

My father died in 1998.

This first volume is dedicated to the political world, drawn across the 70s to the late 90s.

Robin Calvert (son)

March 17 2014

Author of

DR. WHO: MANY HAPPY SOLAR RETURNS,

CLOAK & DAGGER: OPENING GAMBIT &

SUMMER BREEZE: THE SCREENPLAY.

First-class BA, Film/TV Screenwriting, University of Central Lancashire.

BRITISH POLITICIANS

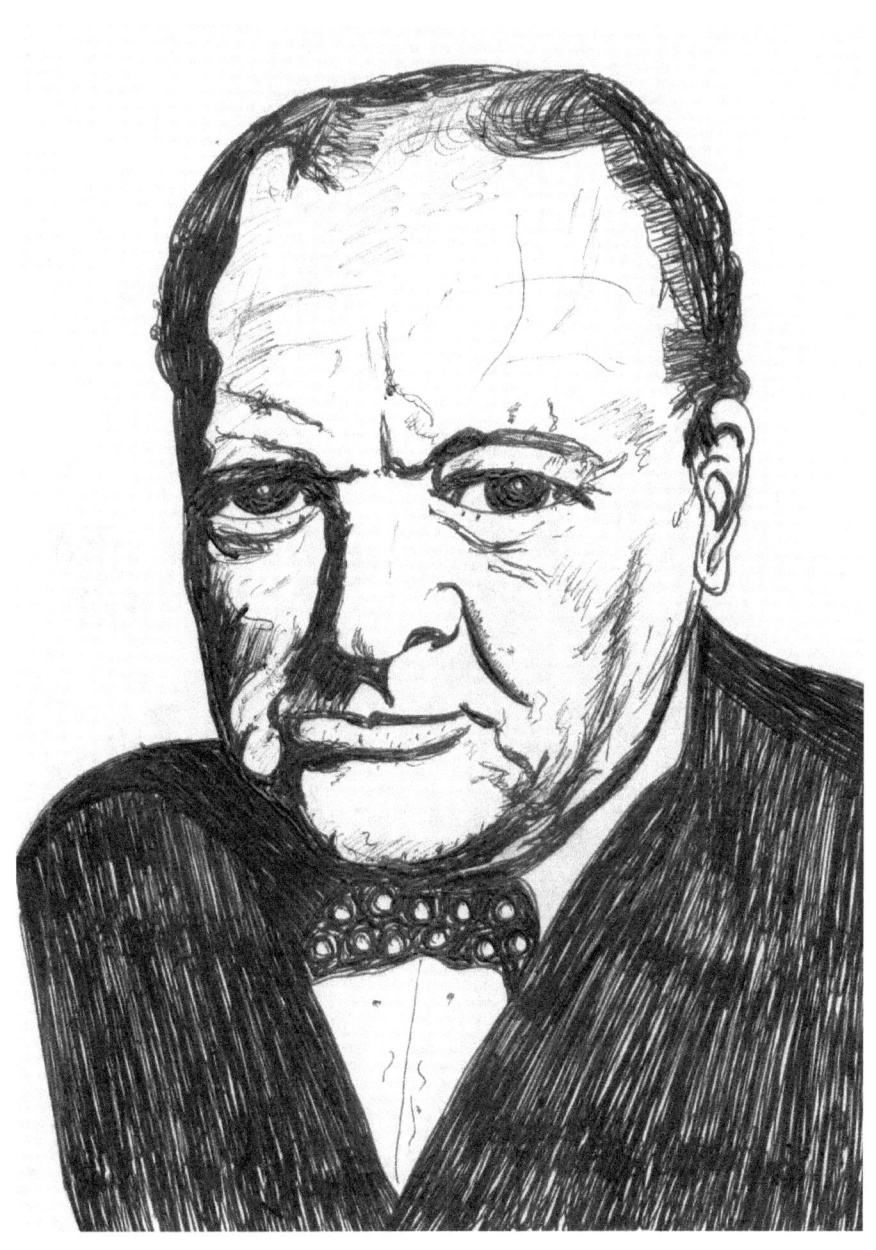

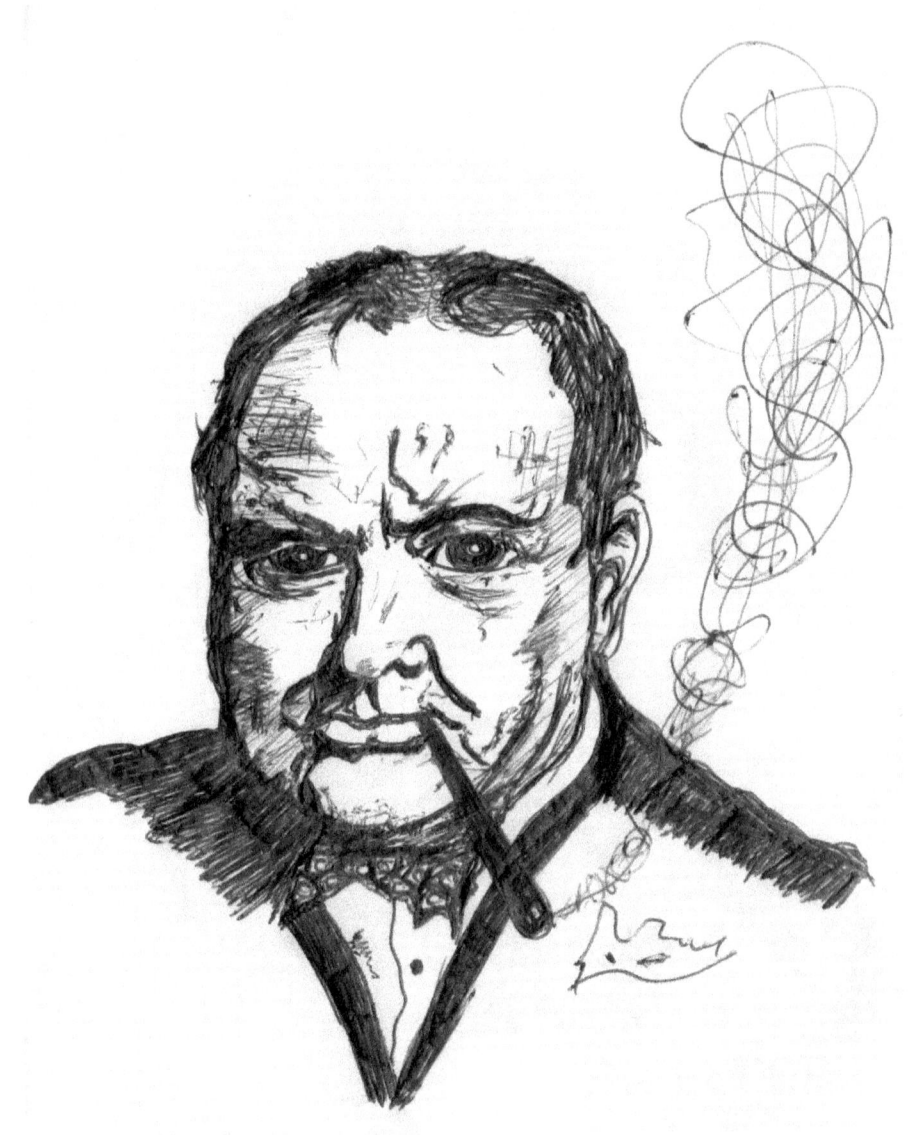

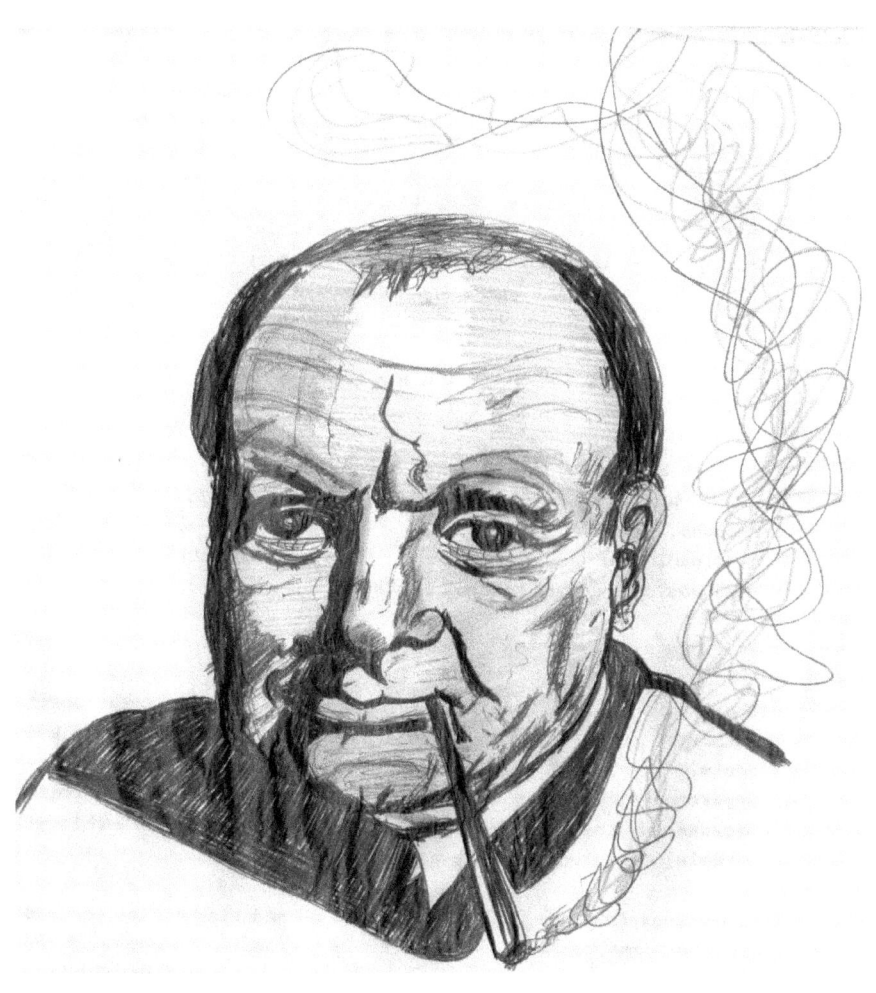

SIR. WINSTON CHURCHILL: First Lord of the Admiralty during the German U-boat attack on the Lusitania, but the right man to be Prime Minister (Tory) during WW2. His 1965 state funeral was a landmark television event.

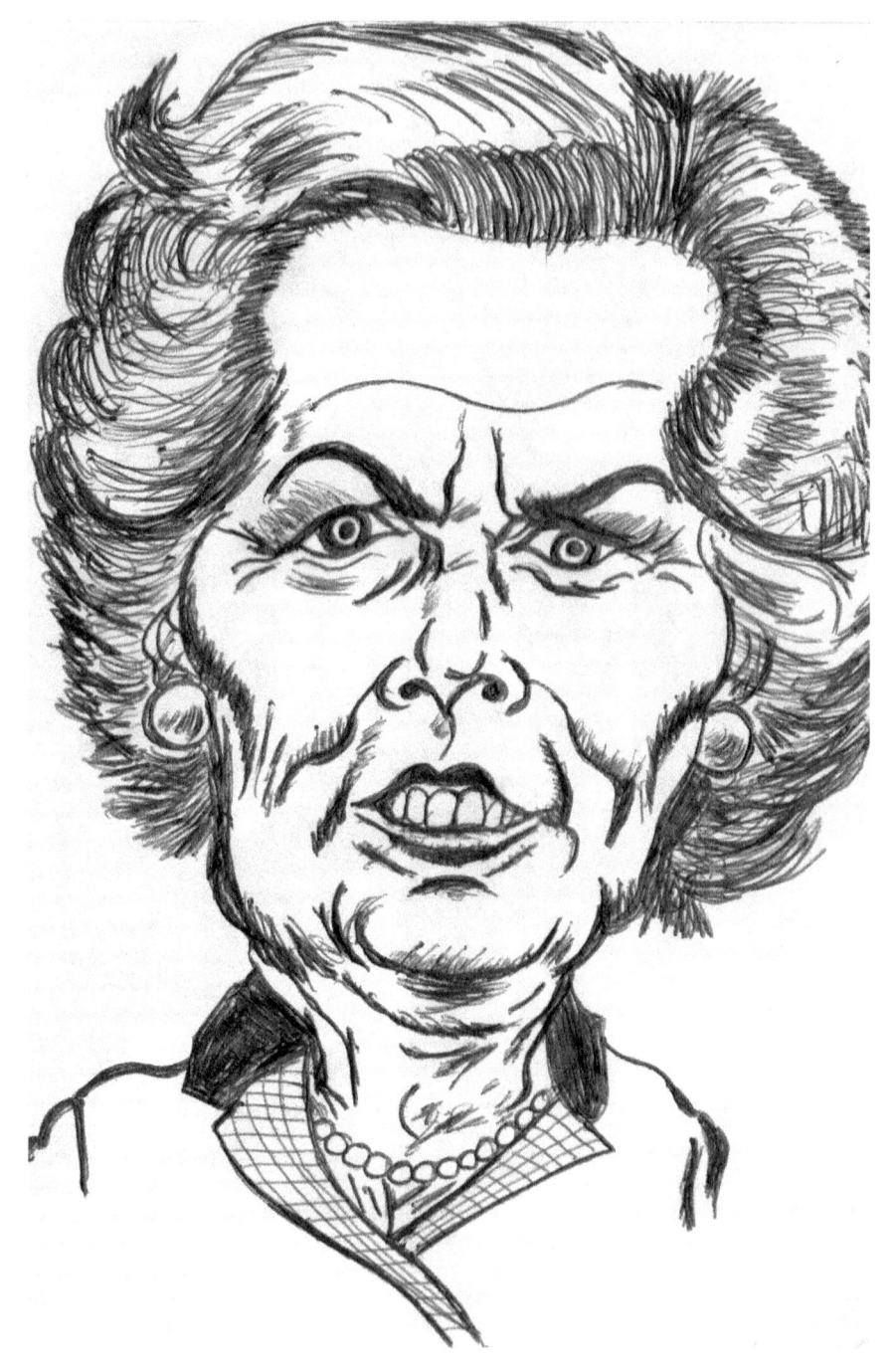

MARGARET THATCHER: Daughter of a grocer, she often disliked the Etonian elite, though married well to businessman Denis Thatcher. Worked her way into Government, but was notorious as "Margaret Thatcher, Milk Snatcher", for ending free school milk whilst Education Minister. She seized on Edward Heath's failure to win the 1974 election over problems with the mining unions and replaced him as party leader in 1975. On becoming the first woman to become Prime Minister in May 1979, she curbed what she felt were excessive union practises, which led to the year long miners' strike of 1983-1984. She also adopted a free-market economy at a time when some traditional industries needed Government assistance to avoid dying off. Loved - particularly on the world stage for the Falklands stand-off - or hated, Thatcher's critics believe she encouraged needless unemployment and exacerbated riots – which returned to undermine her hated poll tax in 1990. Months later, Michael Heseltine challenged her to a vote of confidence in a party ballot. She did not have quite enough votes to win on the first ballot and bitterly recalled how she was coaxed into quitting before the second, after almost twelve years, in November 1990. She died in 2013.

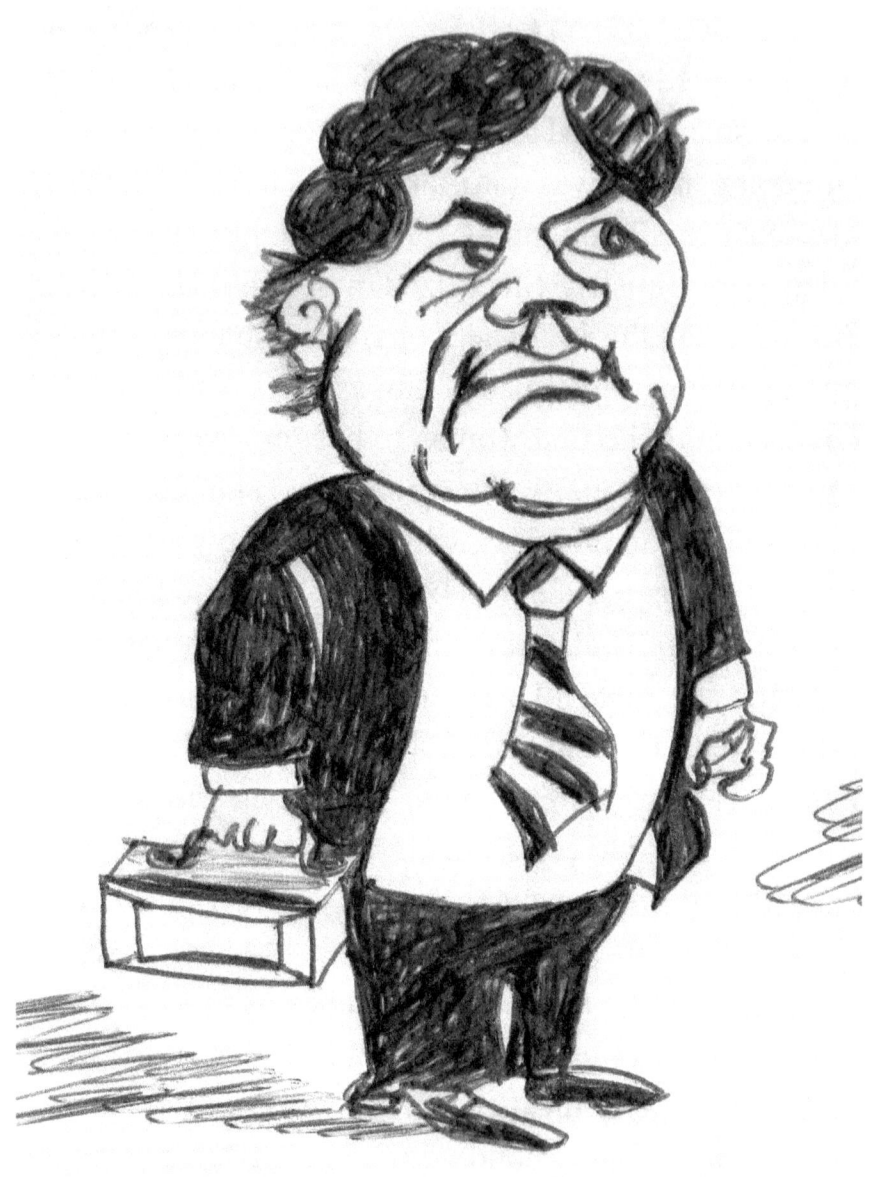

NIGEL LAWSON: Thatcher's Chancellor for much of the 80s. Now sits in the House of Lords as Lord Lawson of Blaby. Father of celebrity chef Nigella.

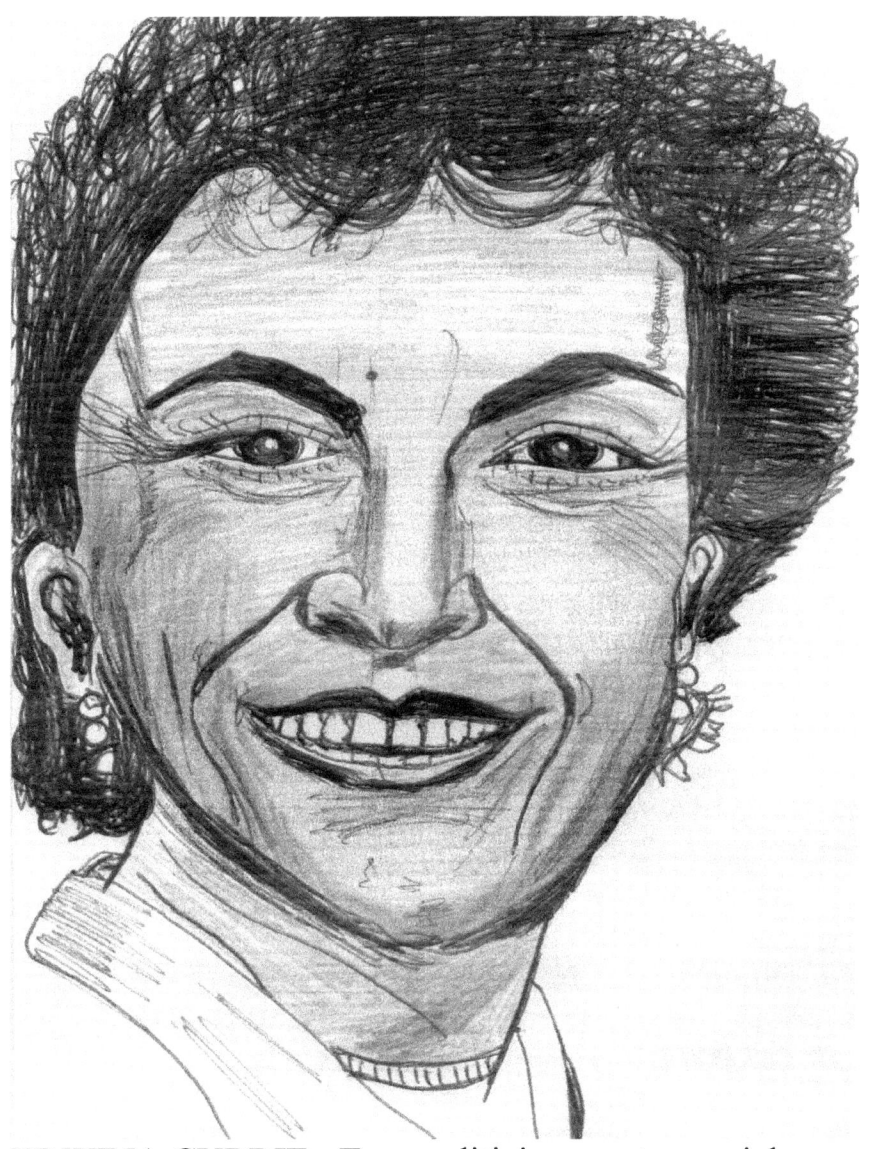

EDWINA CURRIE: Tory politician, controversial over the salmonella affair, but given a new lease of life as a novelist. Her affair with then Prime Minister John Major raised eyebrows some years later.

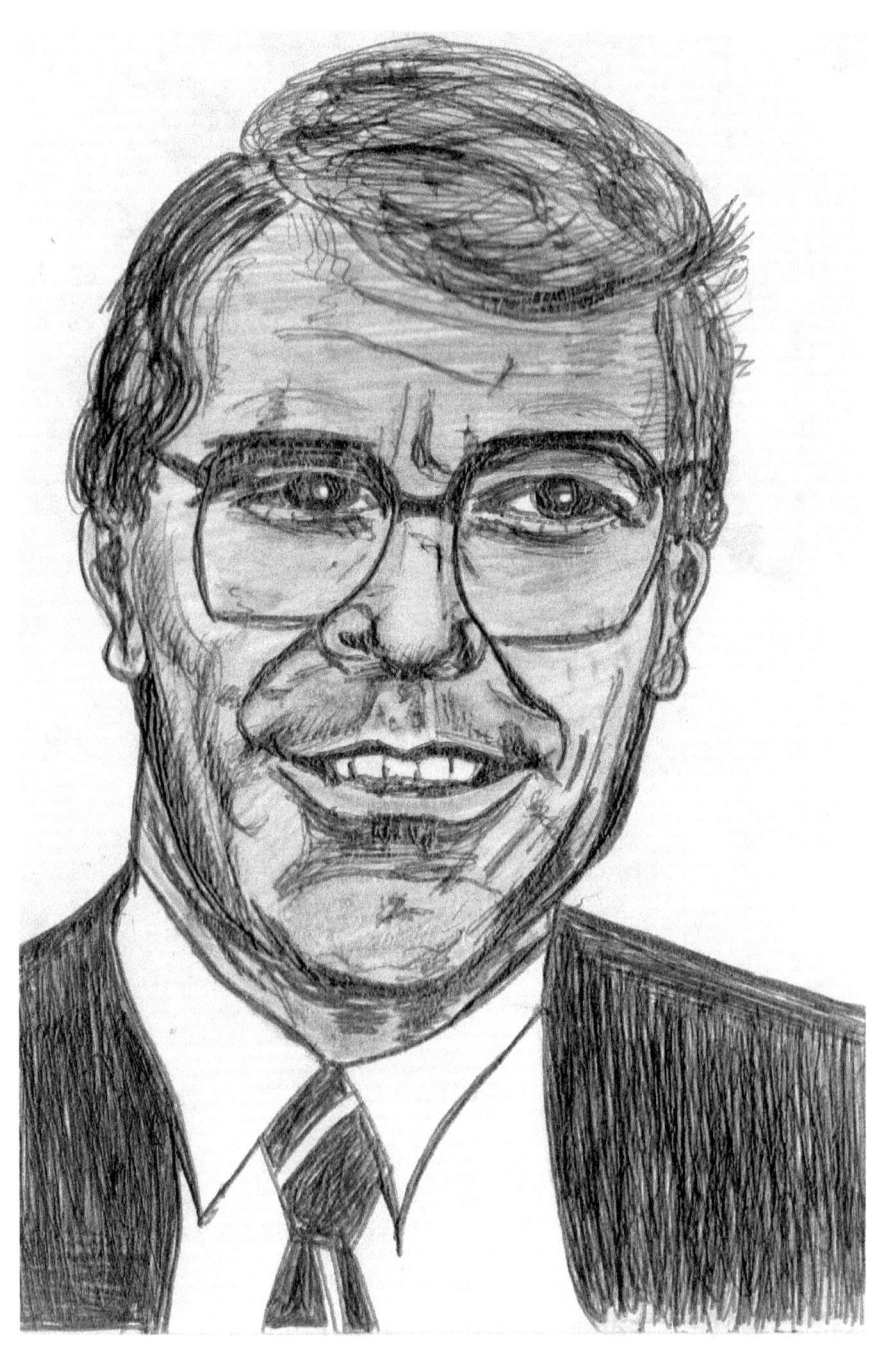

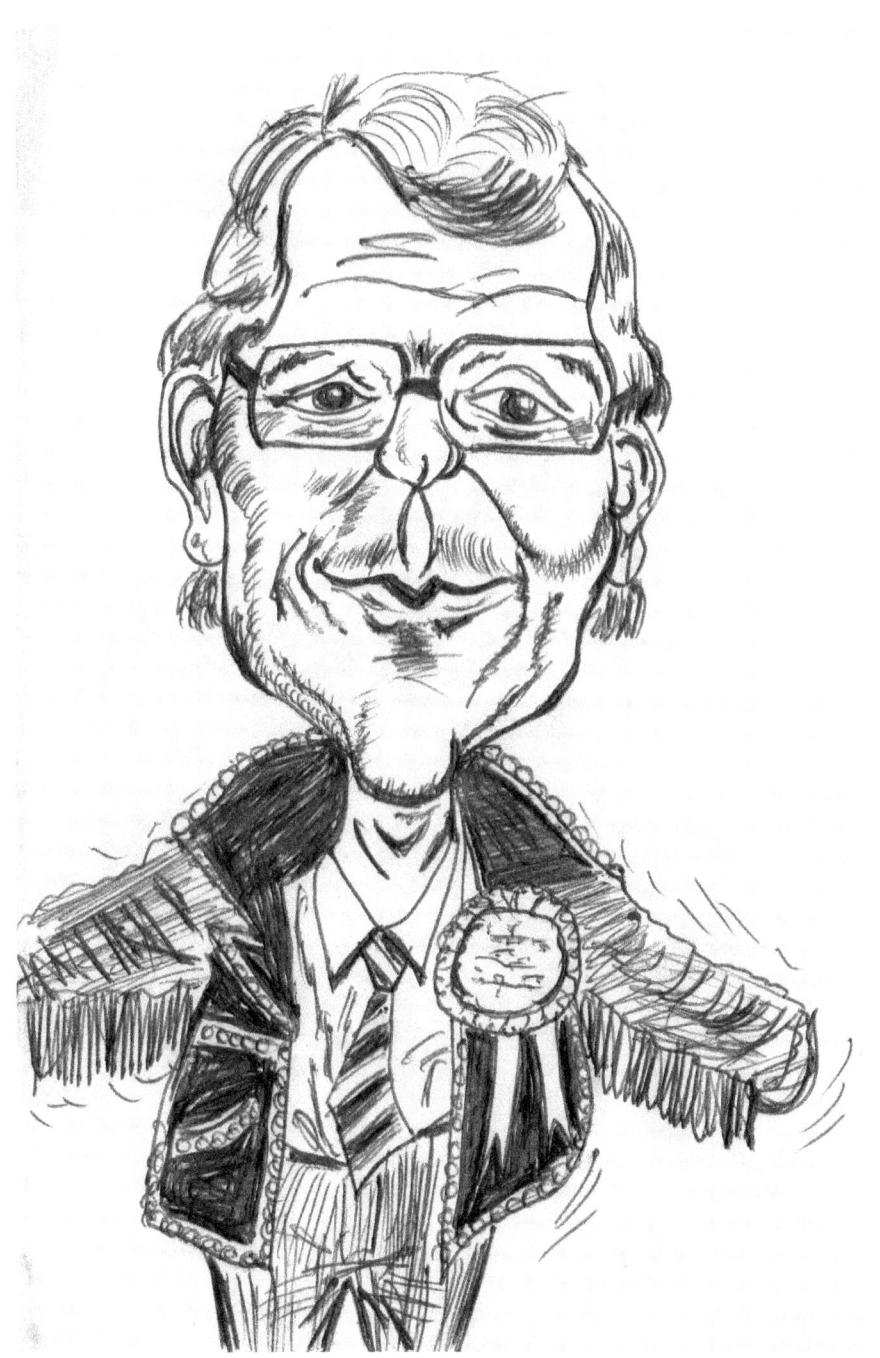

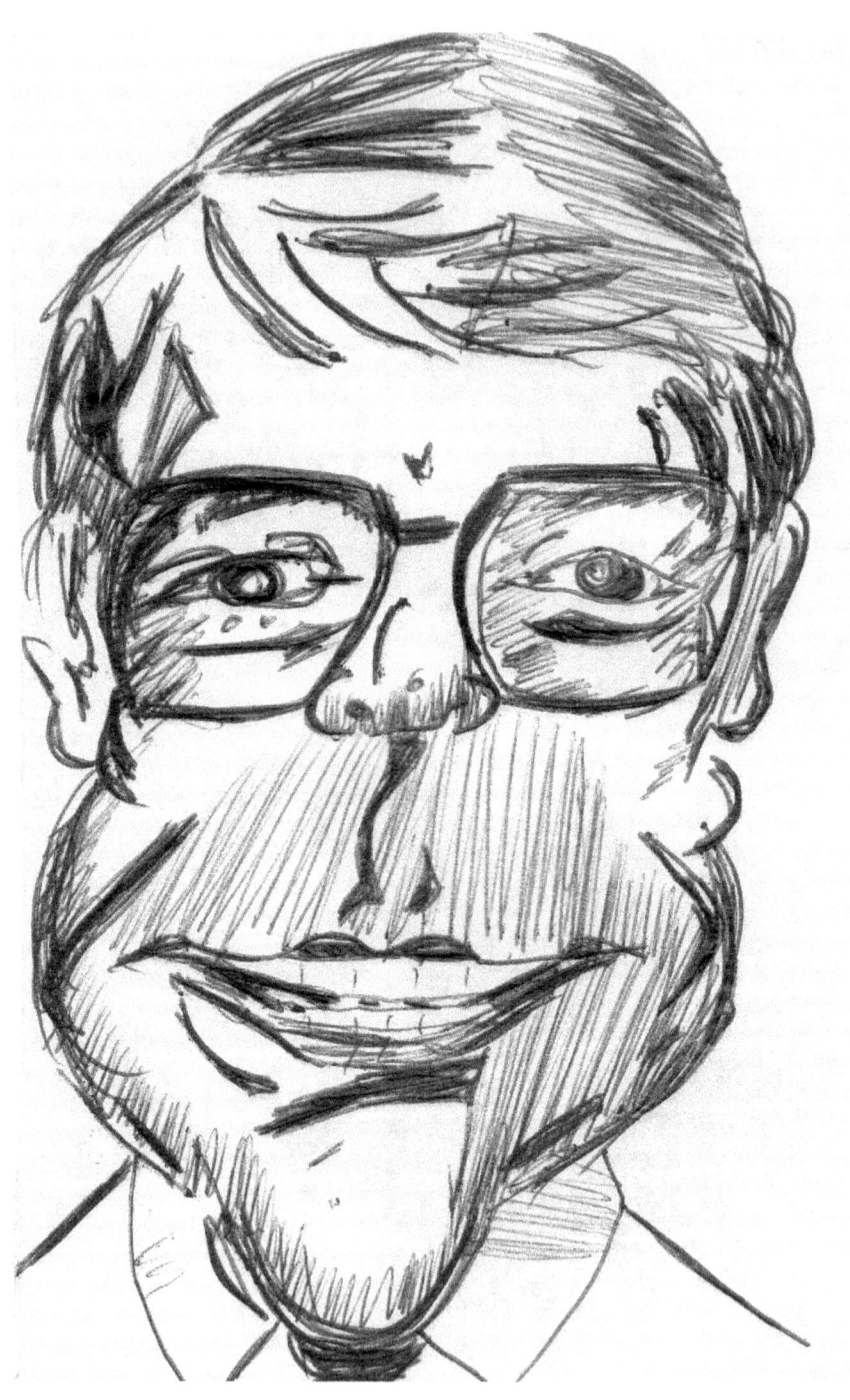

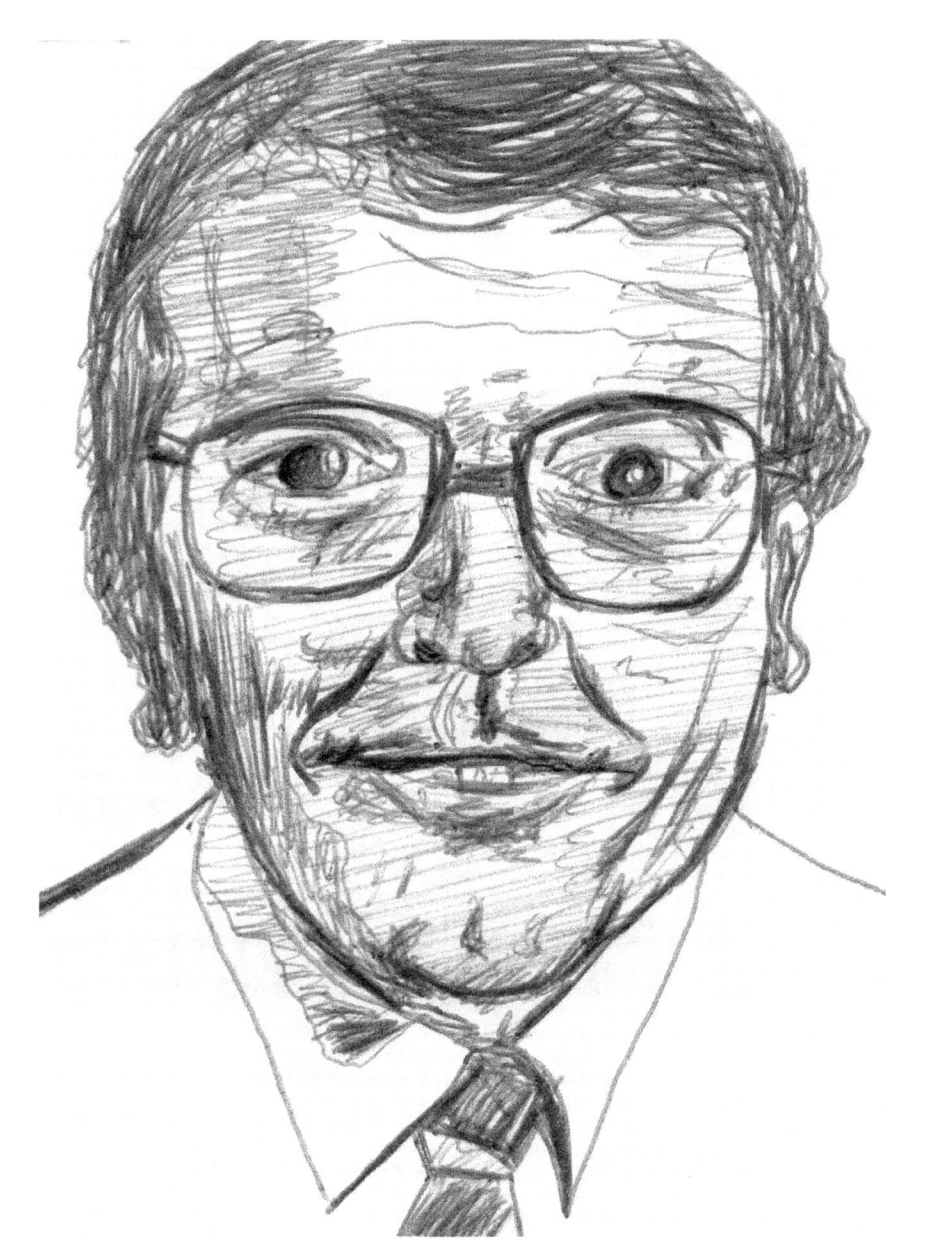

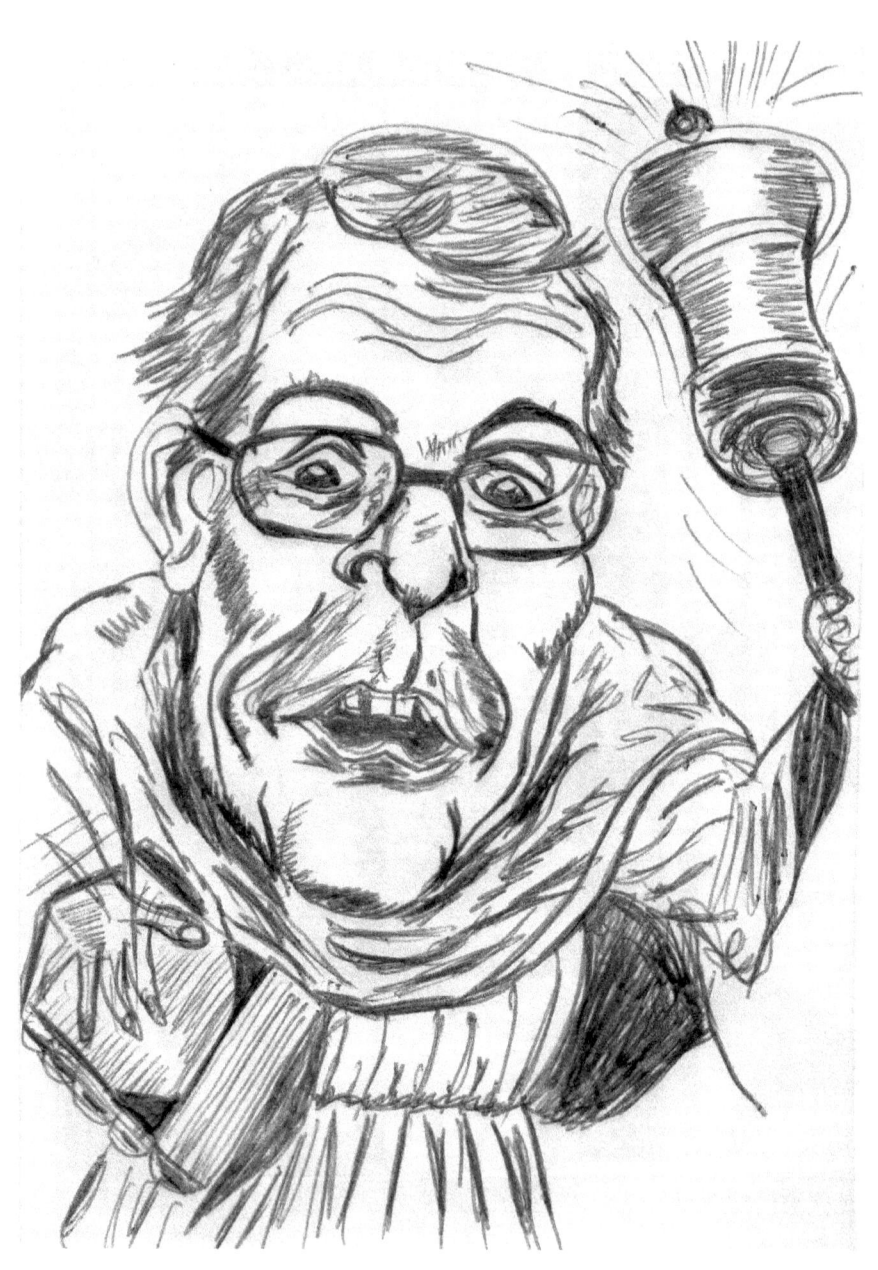

JOHN MAJOR: Tory politician who rose up the ranks of Thatcher's Government rapidly, so that when she stepped down, he was installed as the successful rival candidate for Tory PM against Michael Heseltine's 1990 challenge. While he went on to win the 1992 Election, just months later he presided over the disastrous Black Wednesday affair, which saw the British currency pulled out of the European Exchange Rate Mechanism. However, he faced down Euro-rebel MPs and his own leadership challenge, shoring the majority up with Ulster Unionists, before – holding out to the last possible moment for the next election – he was succeeded by Tony Blair's New Labour in 1997.

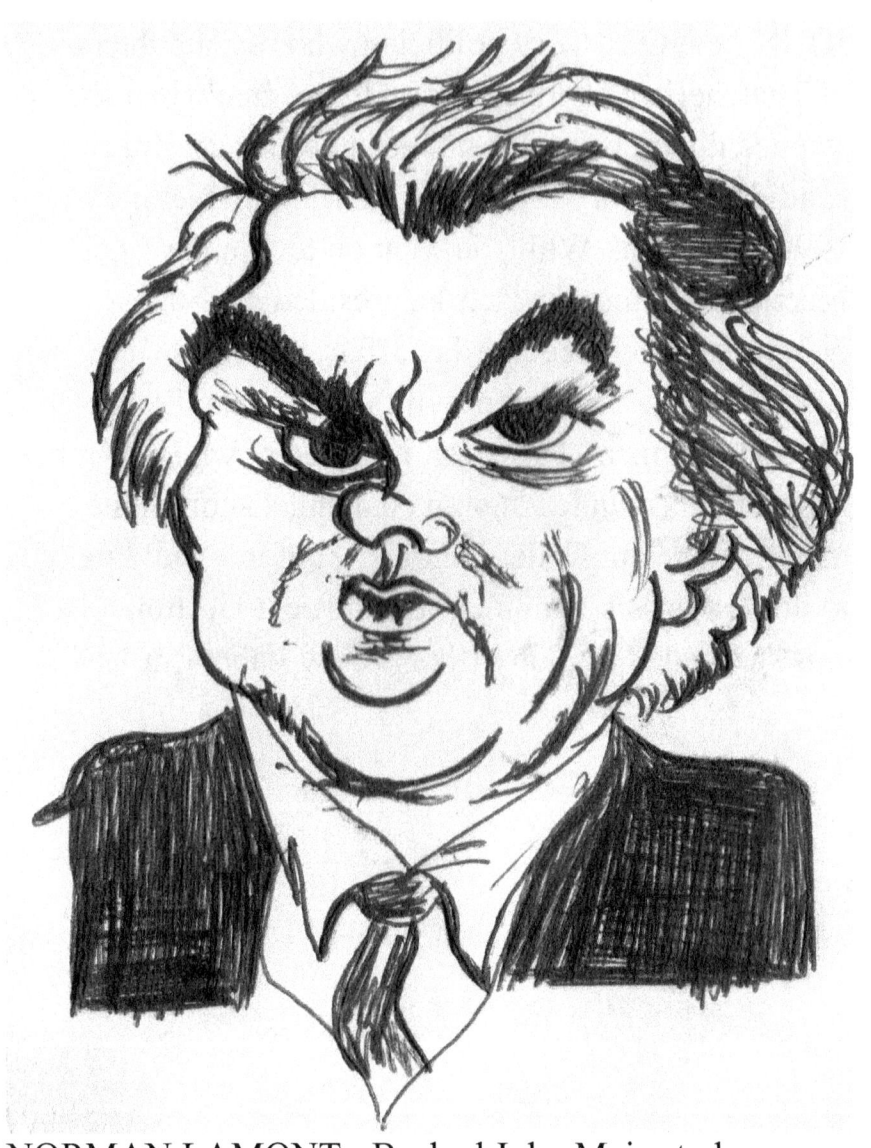

NORMAN LAMONT: Backed John Major to become
Tory PM in 1990, but when replaced as Chancellor
three years later, criticised the Government for seeming
to be in office, not in power.

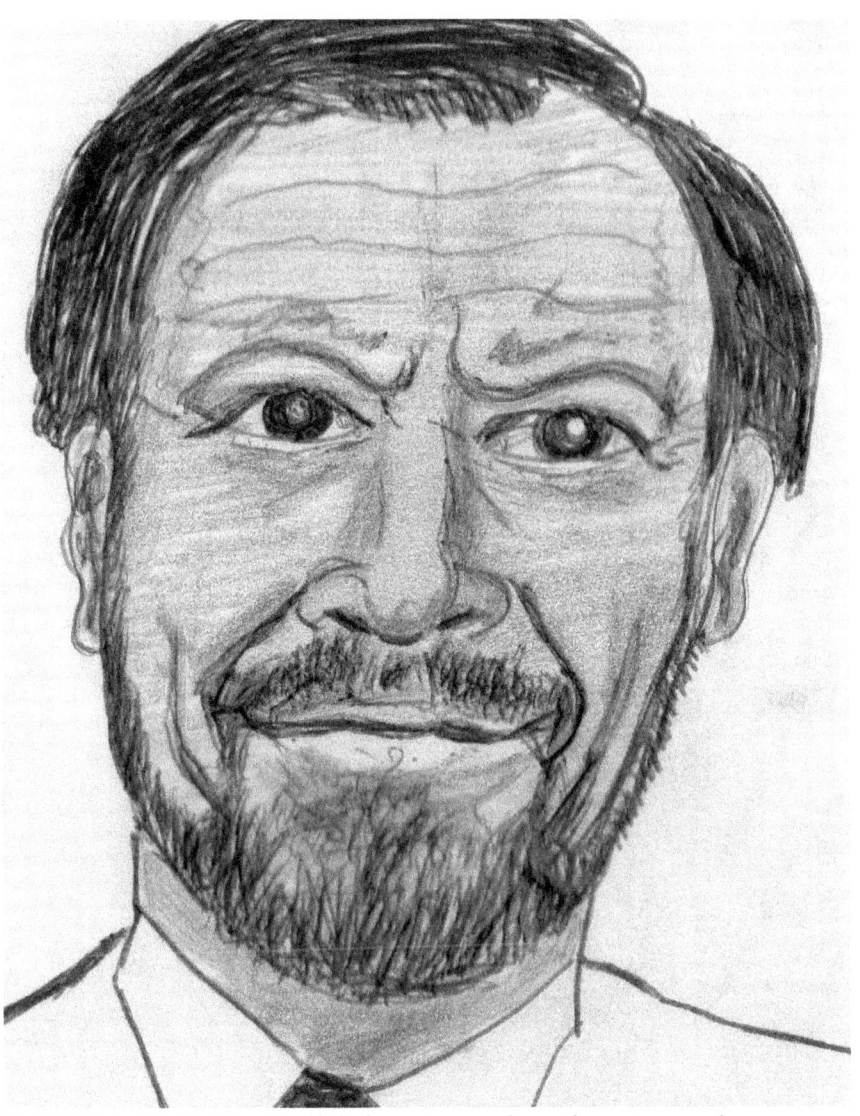

ROBIN COOK: Politician turned author turned
politician again. A former Foreign Secretary (Labour),
his conscience over Iraq saw him quit as Leader of the
House of Commons in 2003. Died of a heart attack
after climbing Ben Stack in Sutherland, 2005.

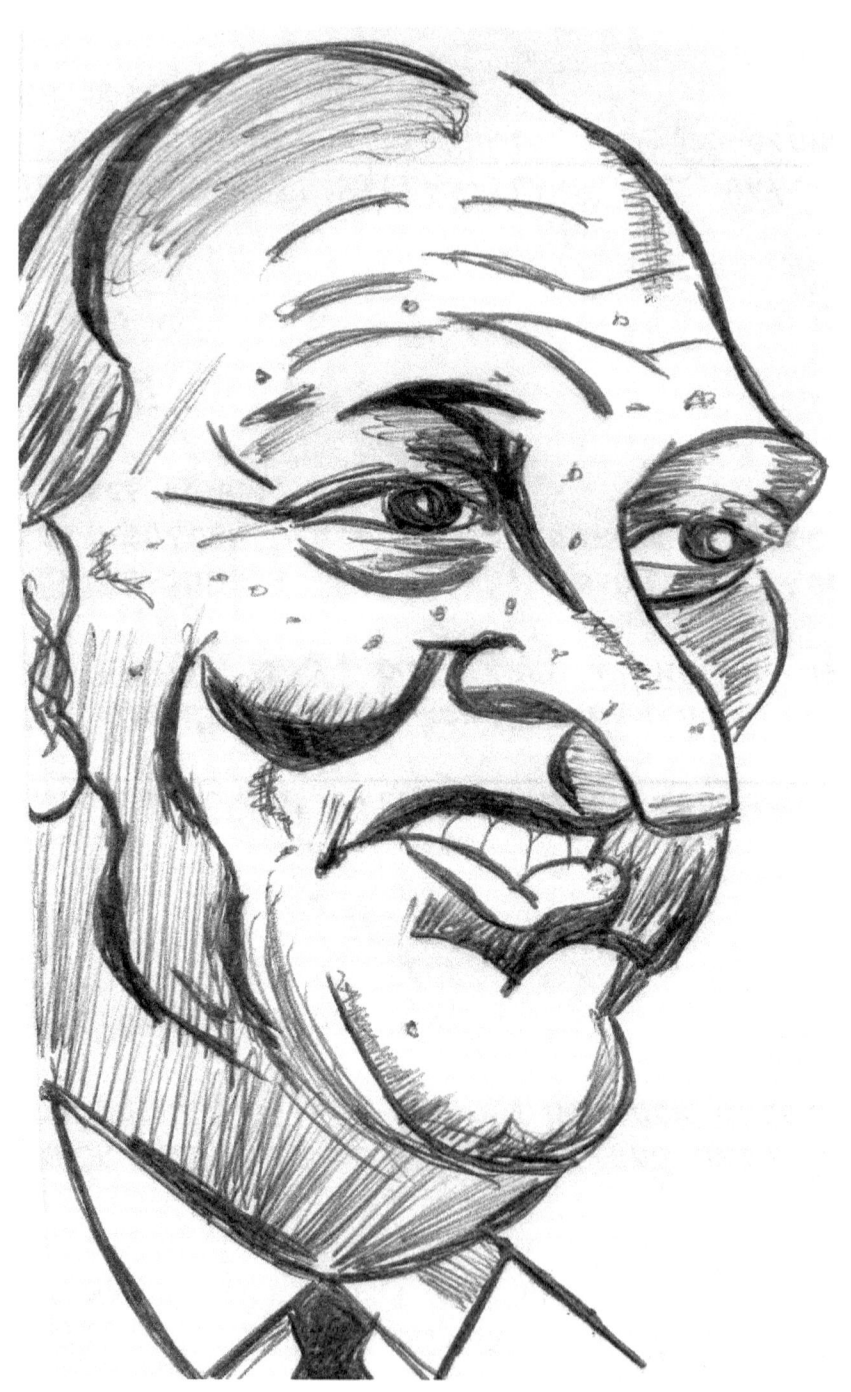

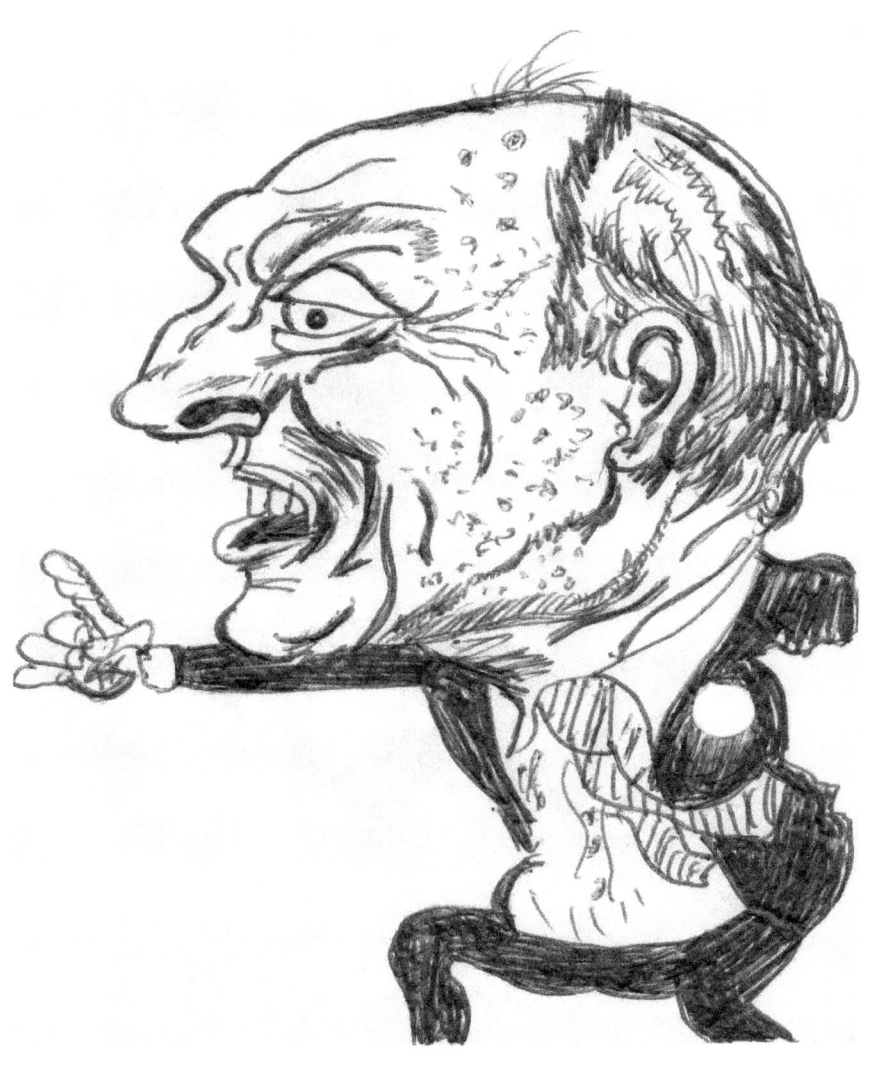

NEIL KINNOCK: This Welsh terrier was Labour Party
Leader between 1983 & 1992 and then became a
European Commissioner and Vice-President of the
European Commission.

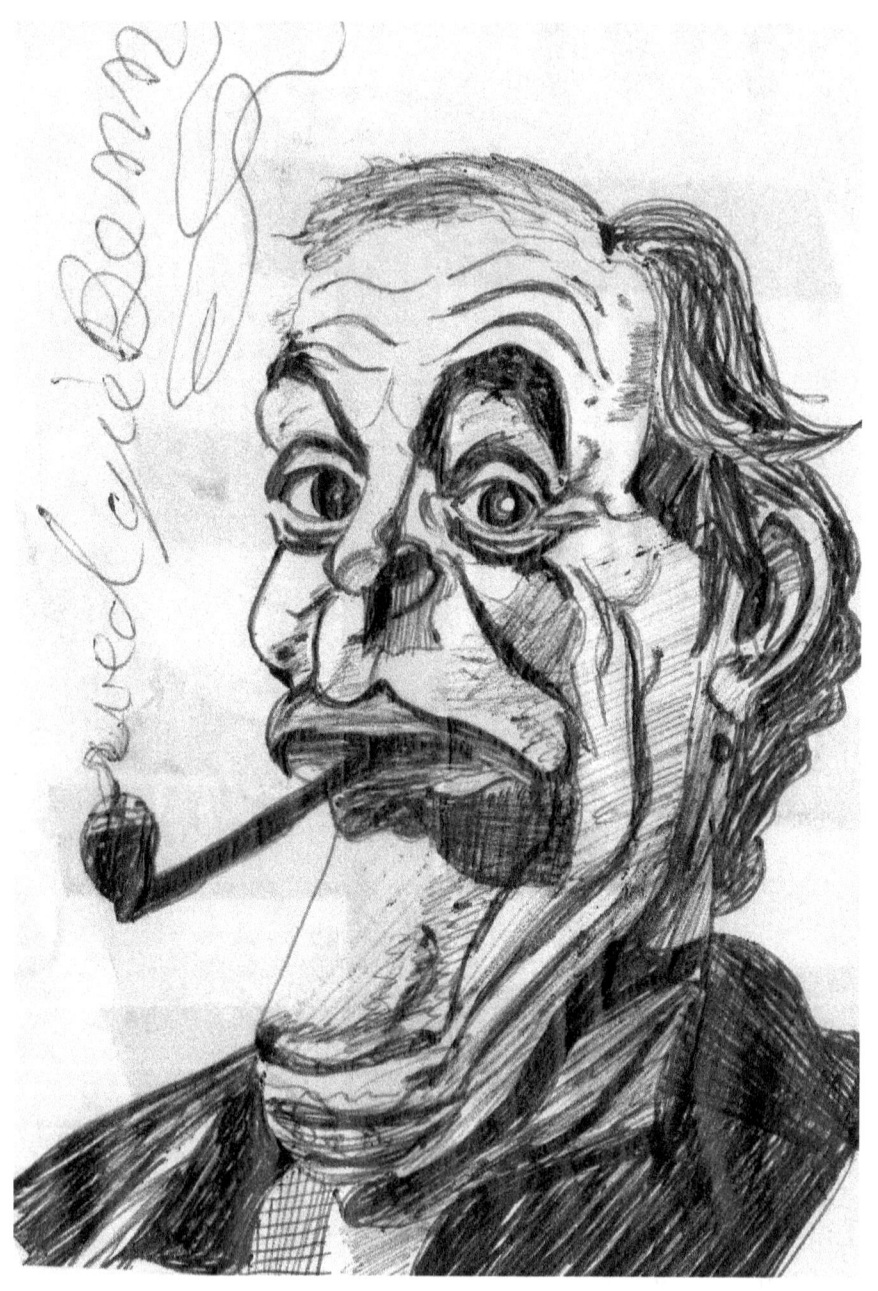

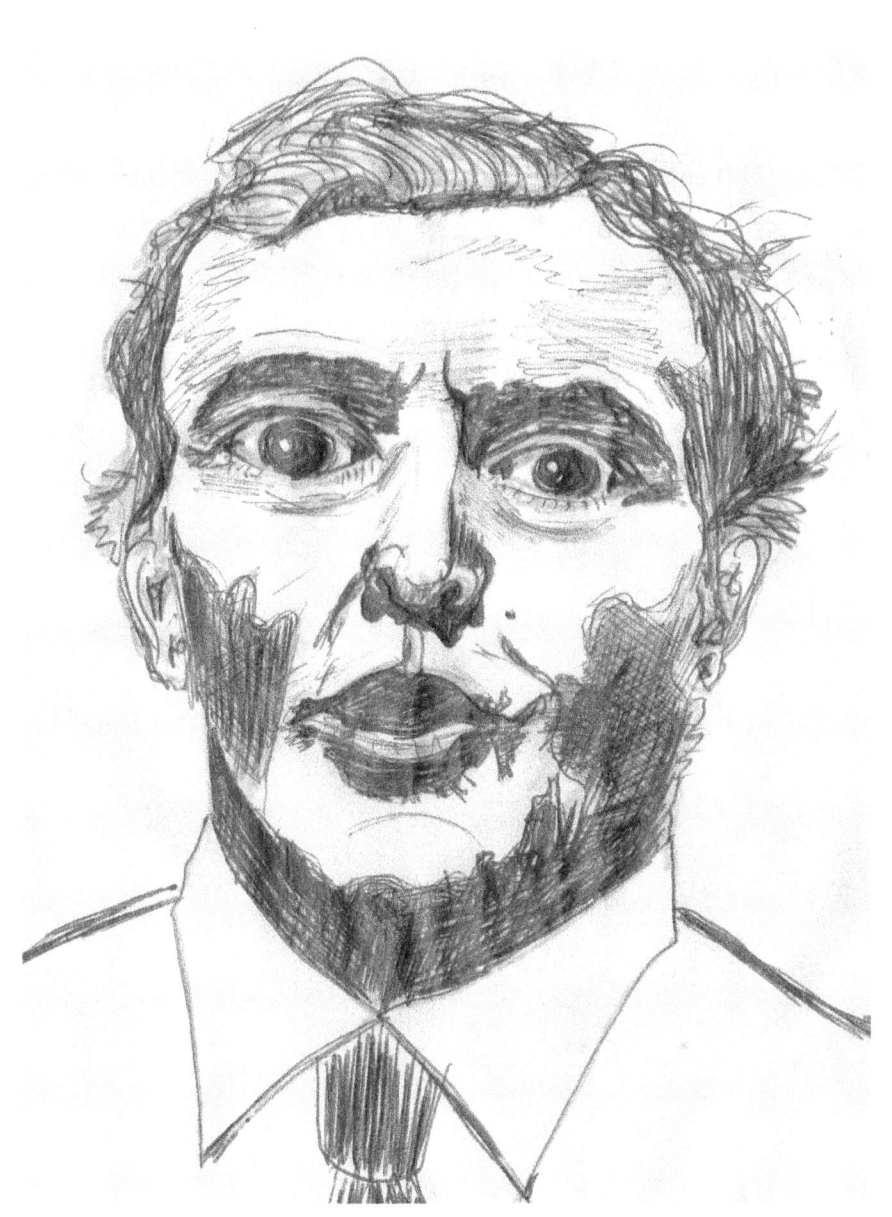

TONY BENN: Born Anthony Wedgewood Benn, upon his father's death and accession to the title of Viscount Stansgate, he found himself barred from the House of Commons. He battled successfully for a change in the law, renounced his title and carried on with his own popular brand of left-wing politics. A fine conversationalist on panel shows such as QUESTION TIME, he was known to be partial to endless cups of tea and a harmless flirtation with Natasha Kaplinsky. Died in 2014.

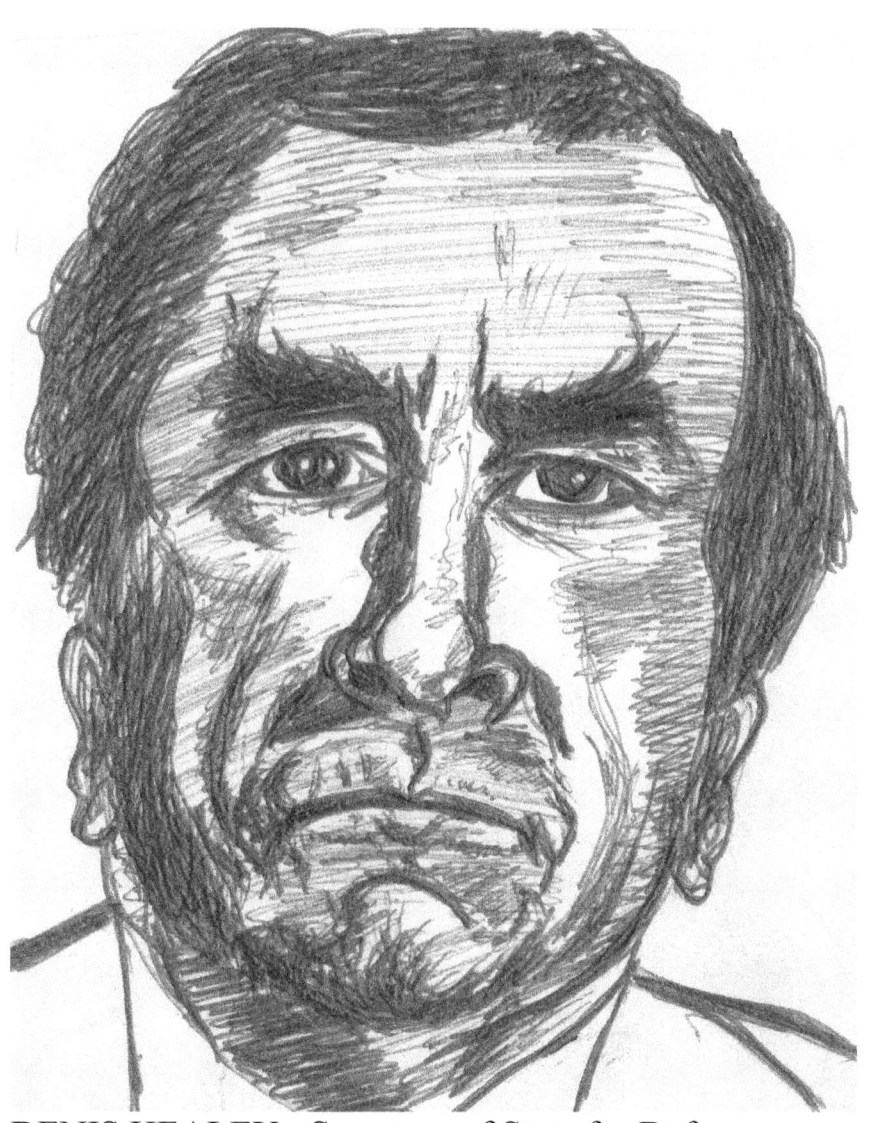

DENIS HEALEY: Secretary of State for Defence (Labour) in the 60s. Chancellor of the Exchequer for Labour in the 70s, infamous for threatening to tax the rich until the pips squeaked. Subsequently, an avuncular figure on radio & TV.

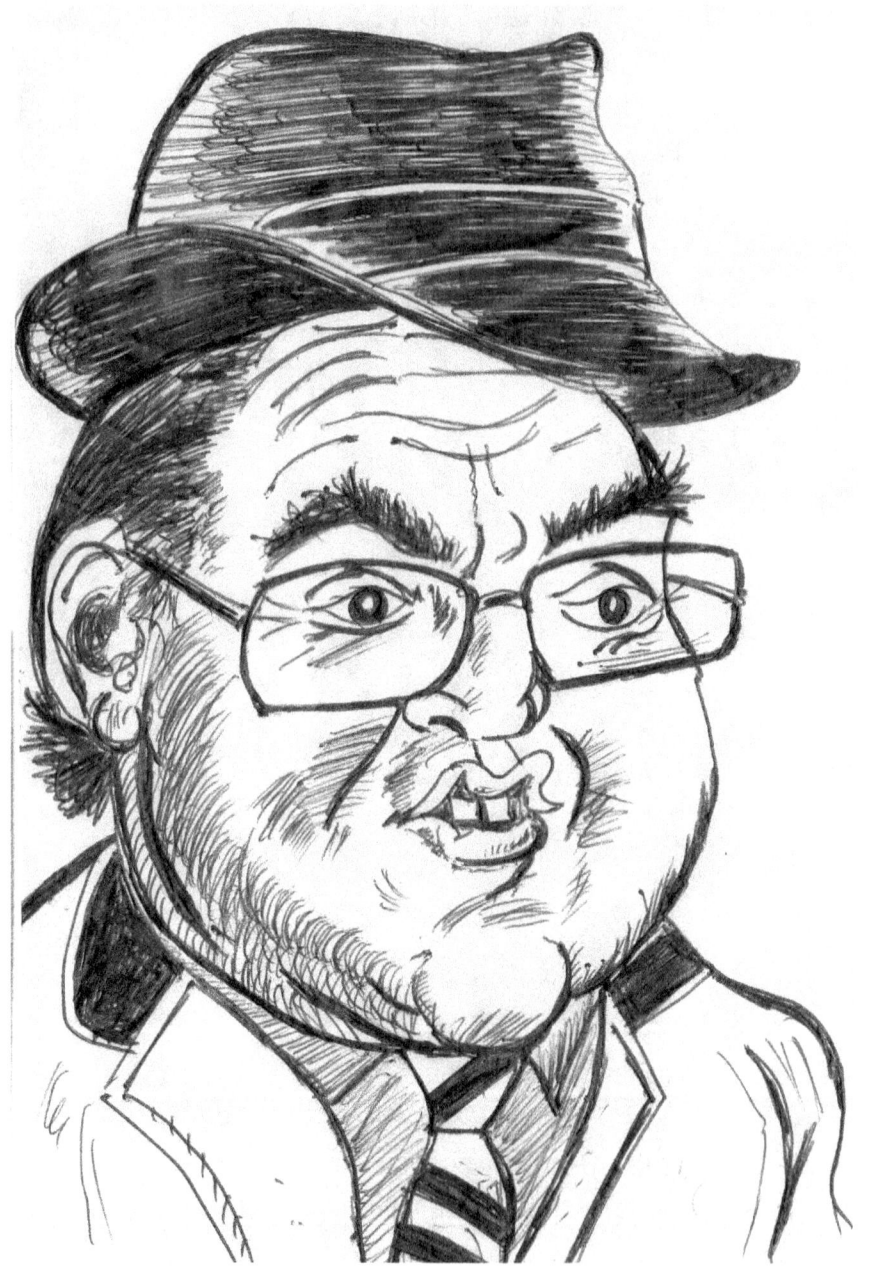

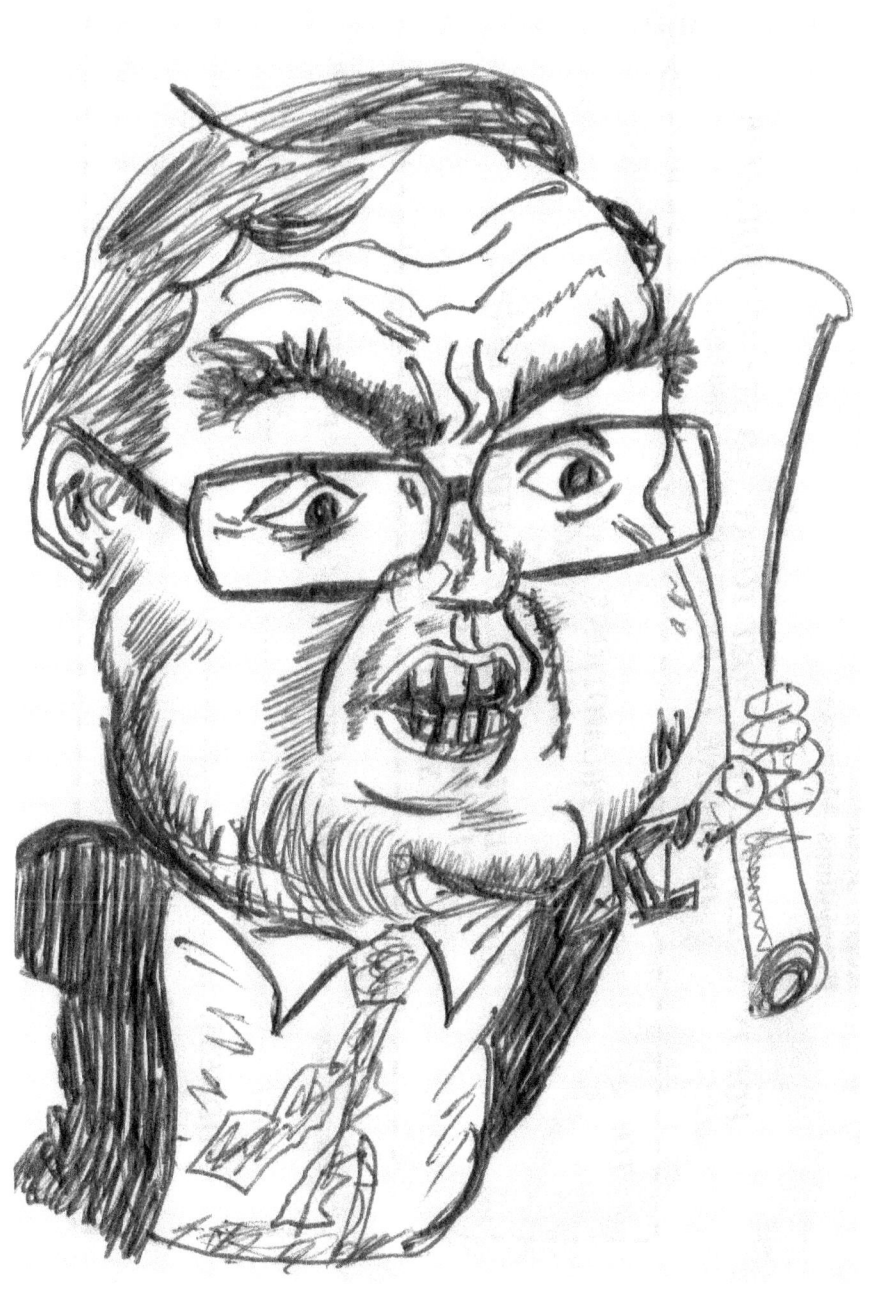

ROY JENKINS: Union official turned Labour MP as Home Secretary, Chancellor and Deputy Leader. He quit the party to set up a more right-wing Gang of Four whose Social Democratic Party merged with the Liberals to ultimately become the Liberal Democrats.

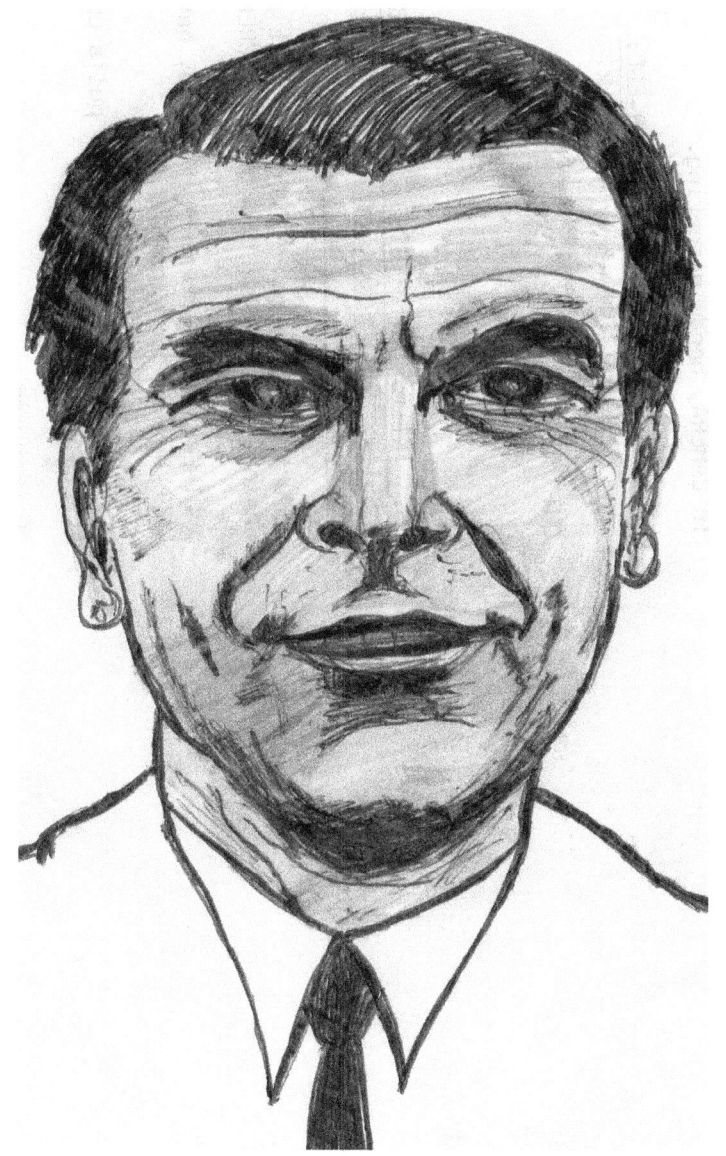

DAVID OWEN: Broke away from Labour as one of
the Gang of Four in 1981, who ultimately entered a
pact with David Steele of the Liberals to form the
Liberal Democrat Party.

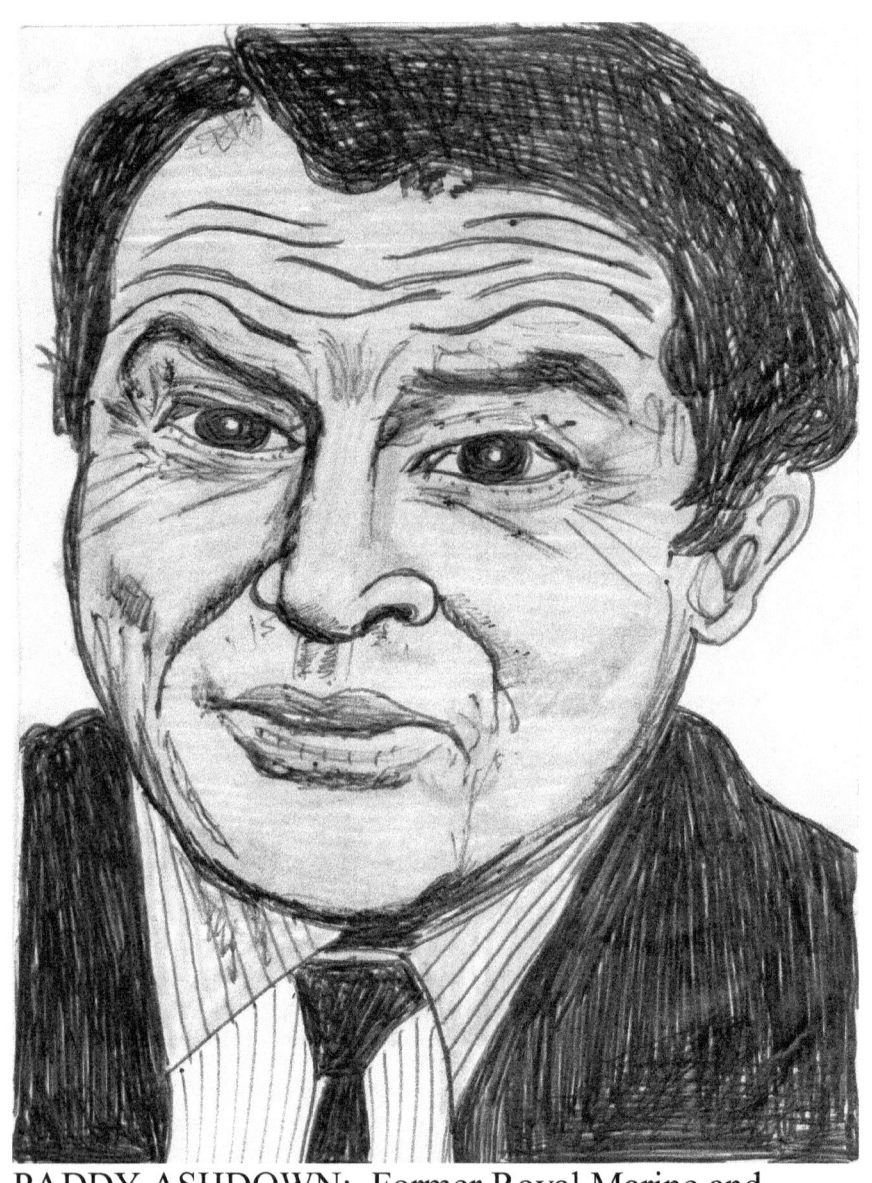

PADDY ASHDOWN: Former Royal Marine and
intelligence officer turned politician. Liberal Democrat
Leader 1988-1999. High Representative for Bosnia &
Herzegovina 2002-2006.

NEWS REPORTERS

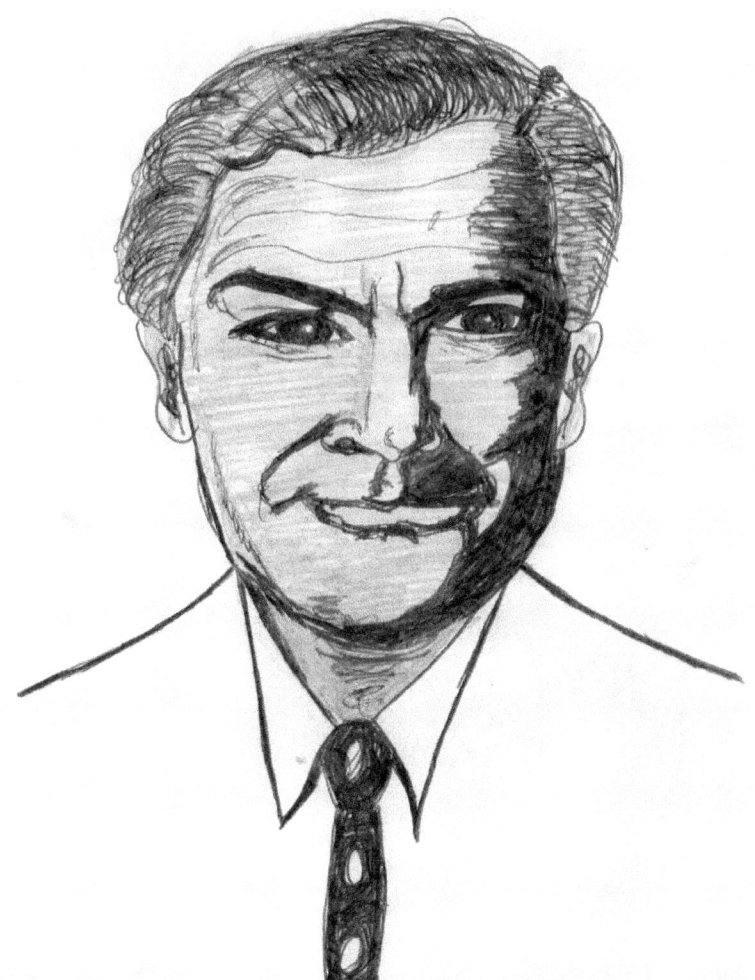

ALISTAIR BURNET: Journalist, editor of the Daily
Express, this Anglicised Scot was doyenne of ITN's
newsreaders from the 60s to the 90s. He also reported
on the Apollo Moon Landing of 1969, general elections
(this time for the BBC) and the wedding of Prince
Charles & Lady Diana (1981).

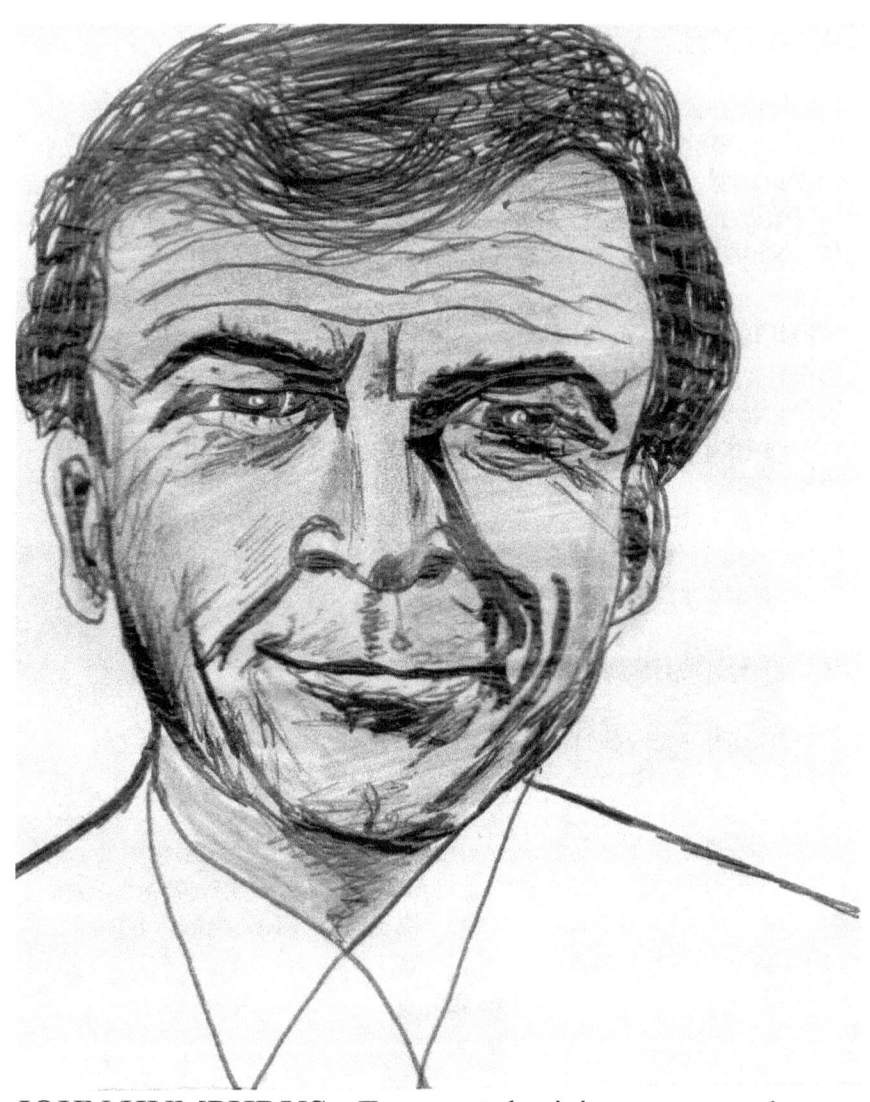

JOHN HUMPHRYS: Earnest television newsreader
who hosts the early morning radio show programme
TODAY, famed for not giving politicians an easy ride.
Elsewhere, took over from Magnus Magnusson as
anchor of MASTERMIND.

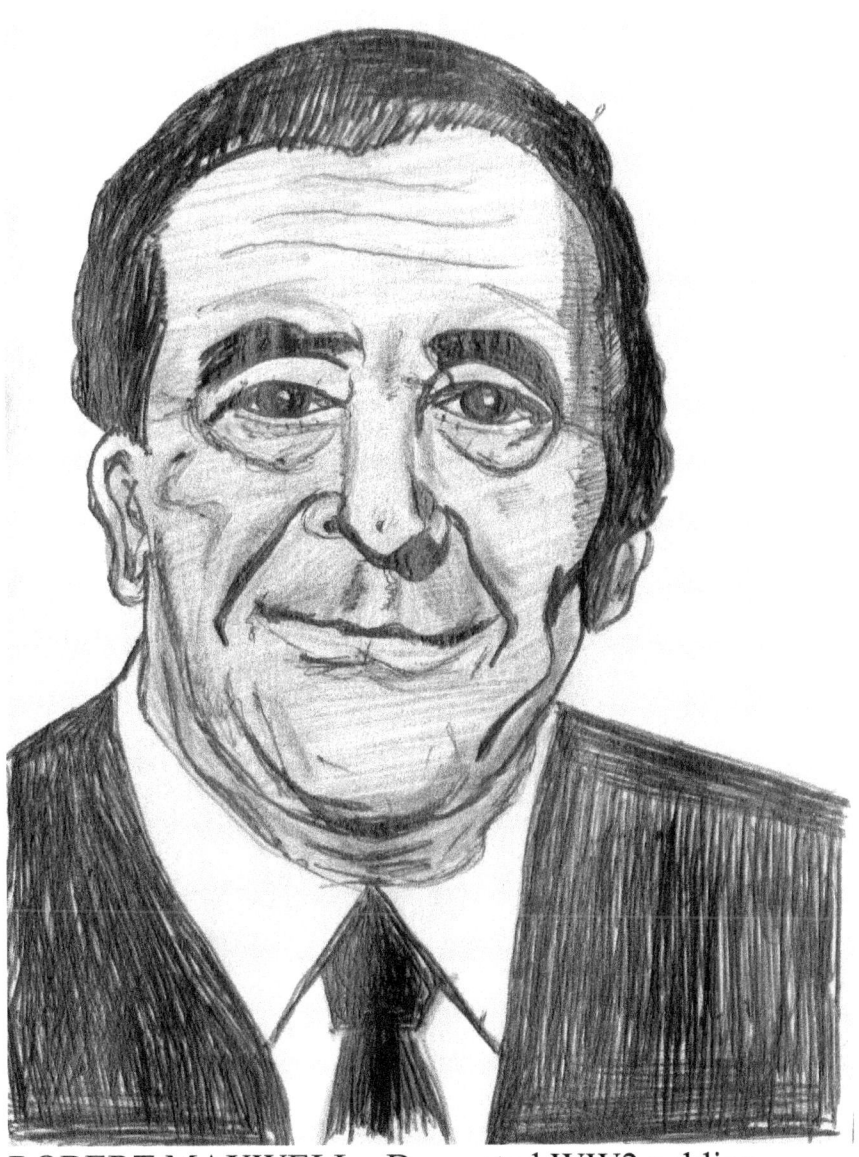

ROBERT MAXWELL: Decorated WW2 soldier
turned publisher & larger-than-life newspaper magnate.
However, his death at sea in 1991 served as a curtain
raiser to financial scandals involving pensions.

THE QUEEN

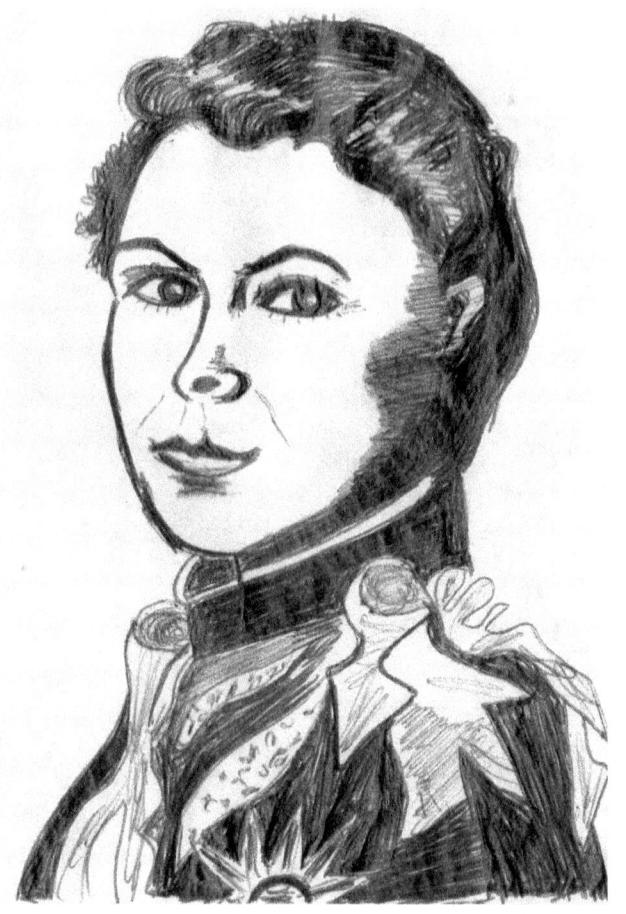

QUEEN ELIZABETH: Following her father's death in 1952, her
State Coronation a year later became the first major television event
for the general public. For more than any previous Monarch,
Elizabeth sought to connect with her subjects. Married to Prince
Philip, her childrens' marriages haven't always gone to plan, but she
remains a popular figure through all her Jubilee celebrations and
happily presides over a resurgent Royal Family.

AMERICAN POLITICIANS

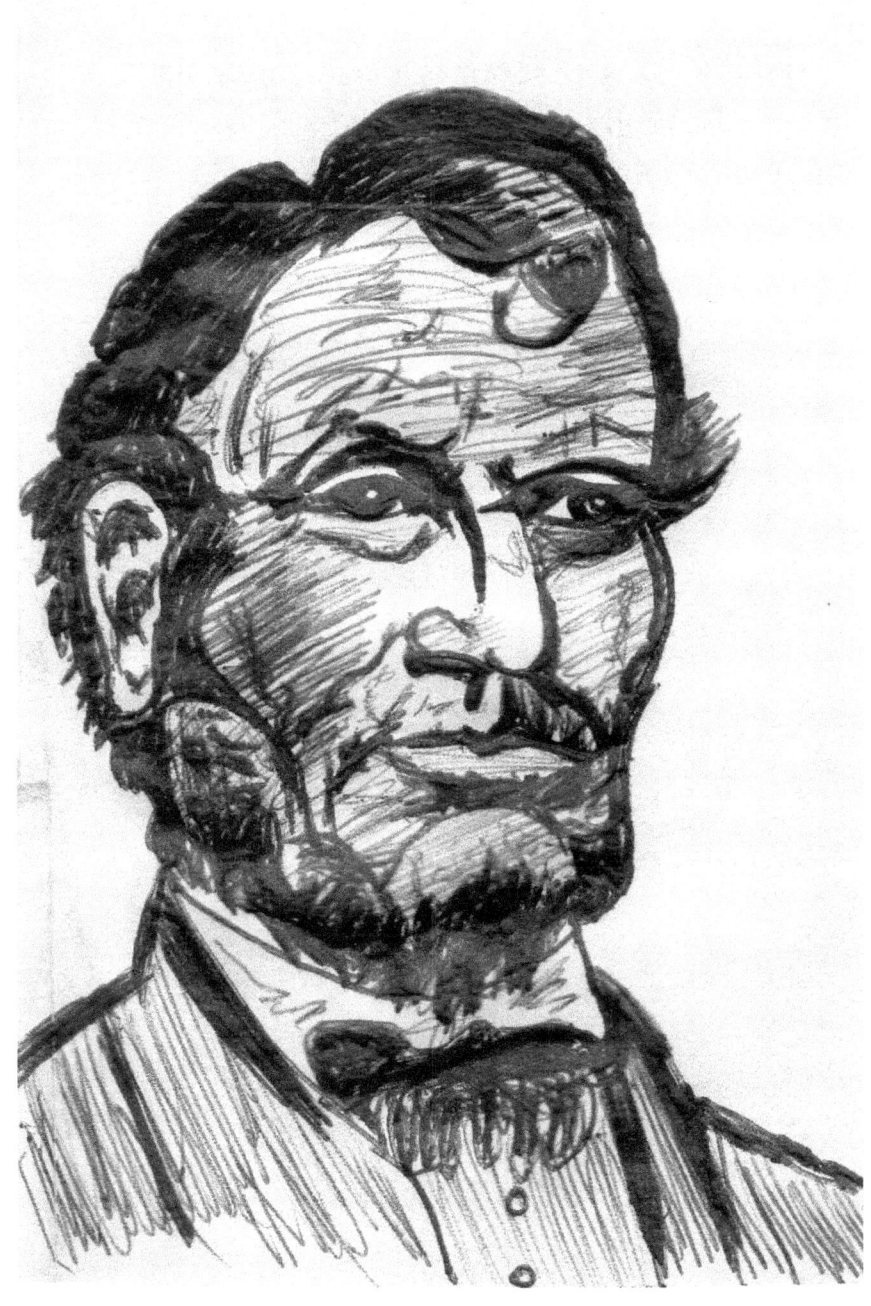

ABRAHAM LINCOLN (above): US President who saw out the Civil War, preserving the Union with the Gettysburg Address. Seen as a moderniser, not least through the abolition of slavery, he was assassinated in a theatre by John Wilkes Booth (1885).

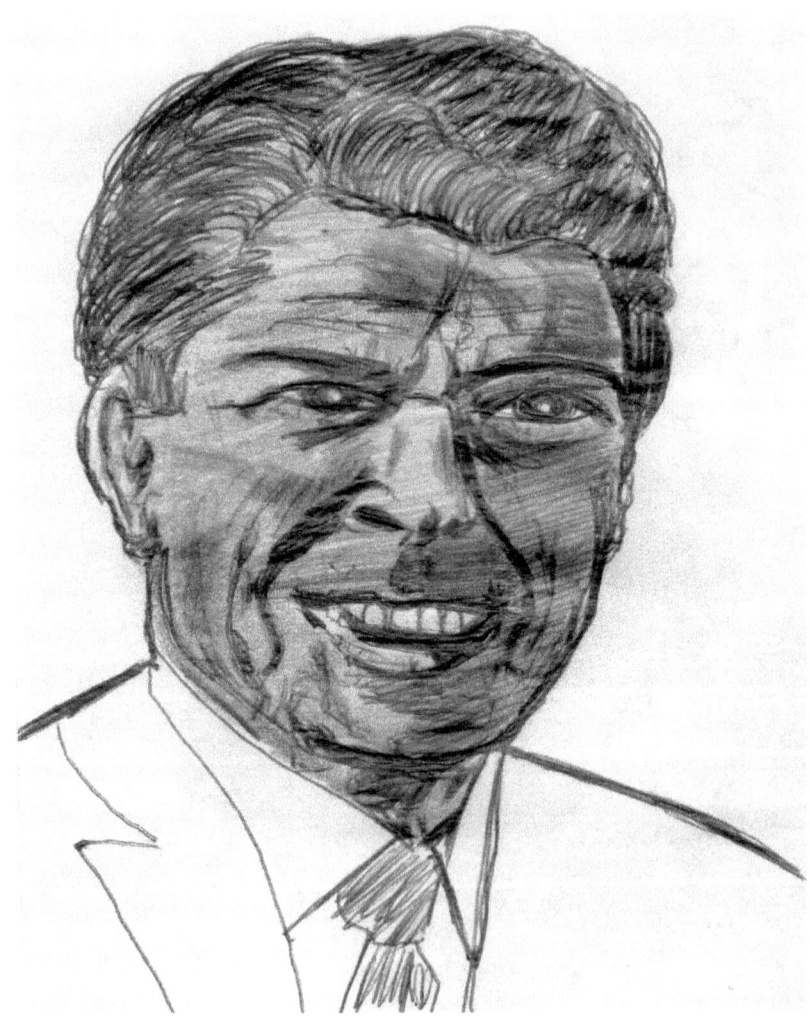

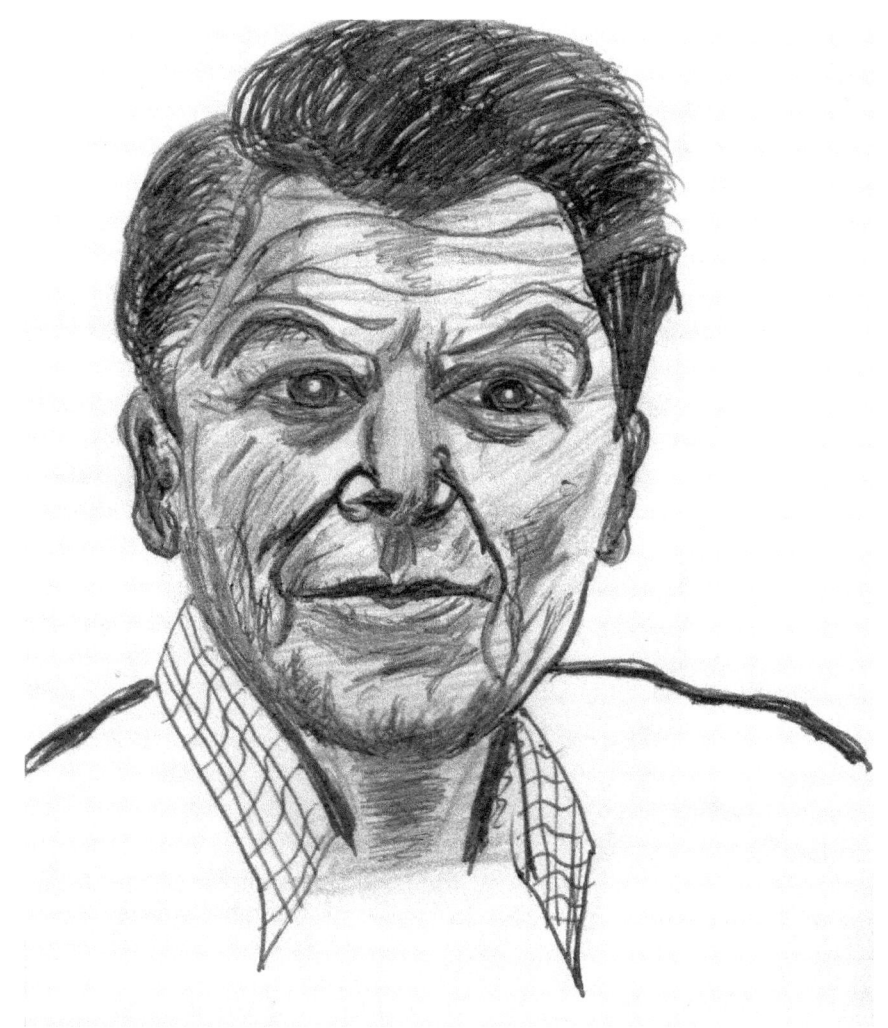

RONALD REAGAN: Popular American film star of
the 40s & 50s, who quit to become Governor of
California and then US President in 1981. He survived
an assassination attempt, bombed Libya and sought to
broker peace to end the Cold War with Russia. Latterly
suffered Alzheimer's disease.

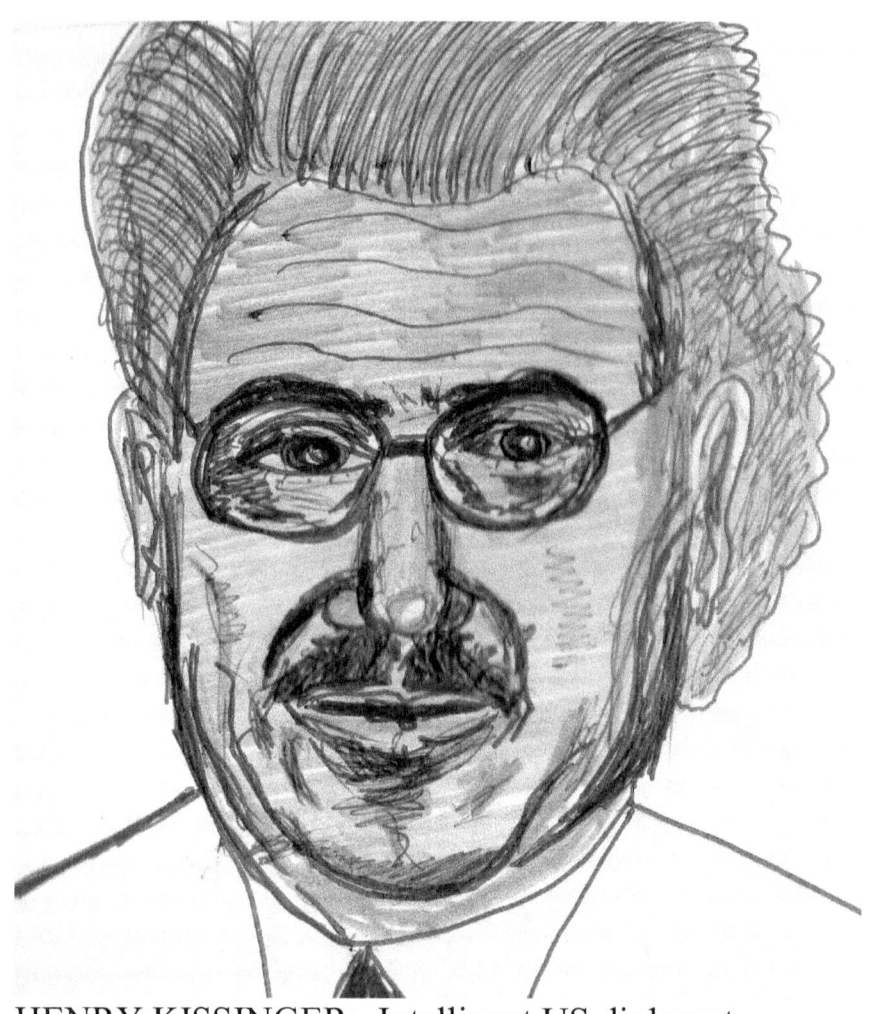

HENRY KISSINGER: Intelligent US diplomat, National Security Adviser and Secretary of State who eventually pulled for withdrawal from Vietnam and had a detente approach to Russia & China. Influence much sought.

POLITICIANS FROM OTHER NATIONS

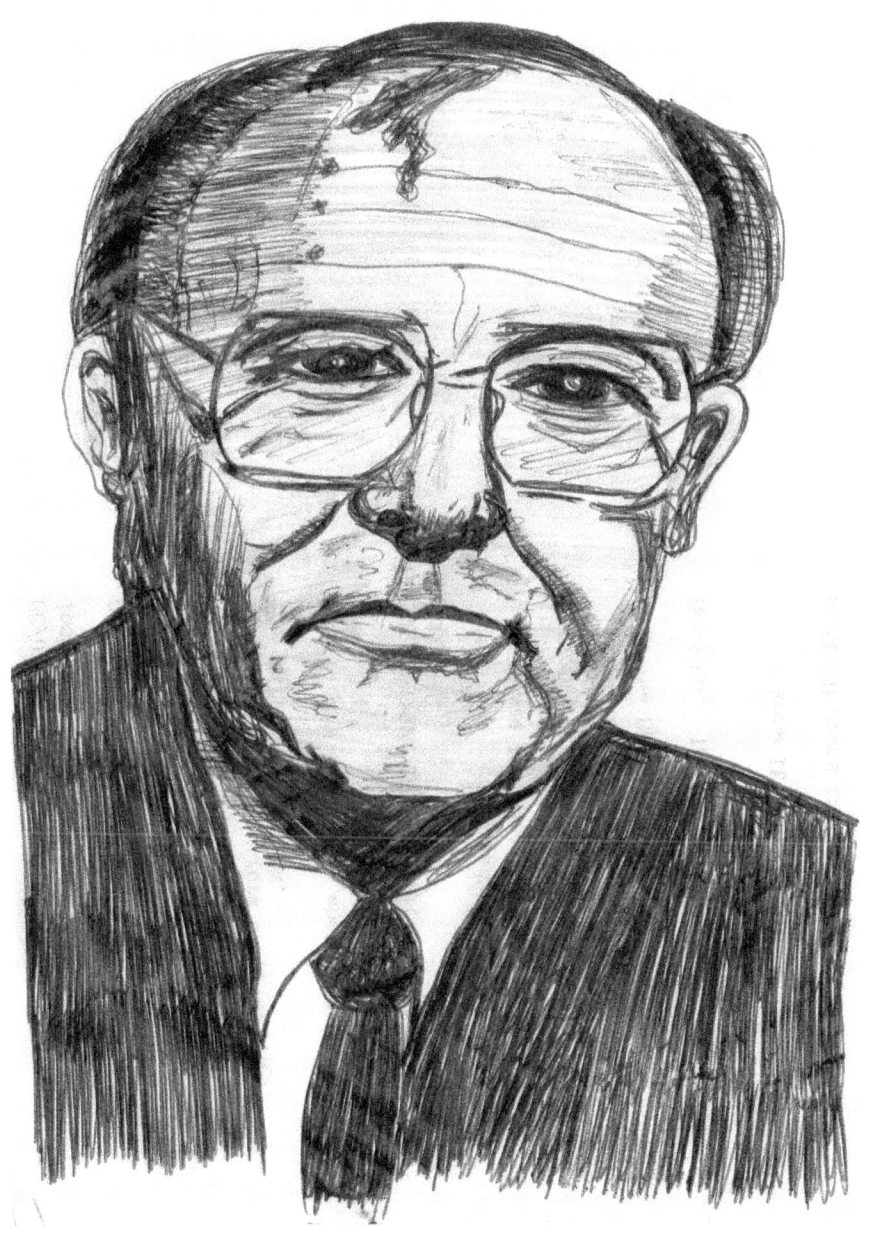

MIKHAIL GORBACHEV (above): Last leader of the old Soviet Union until 1991 during the glasnost period which effectively thawed the Cold War. He, Reagan & Thatcher comprised a hopeful trinity.

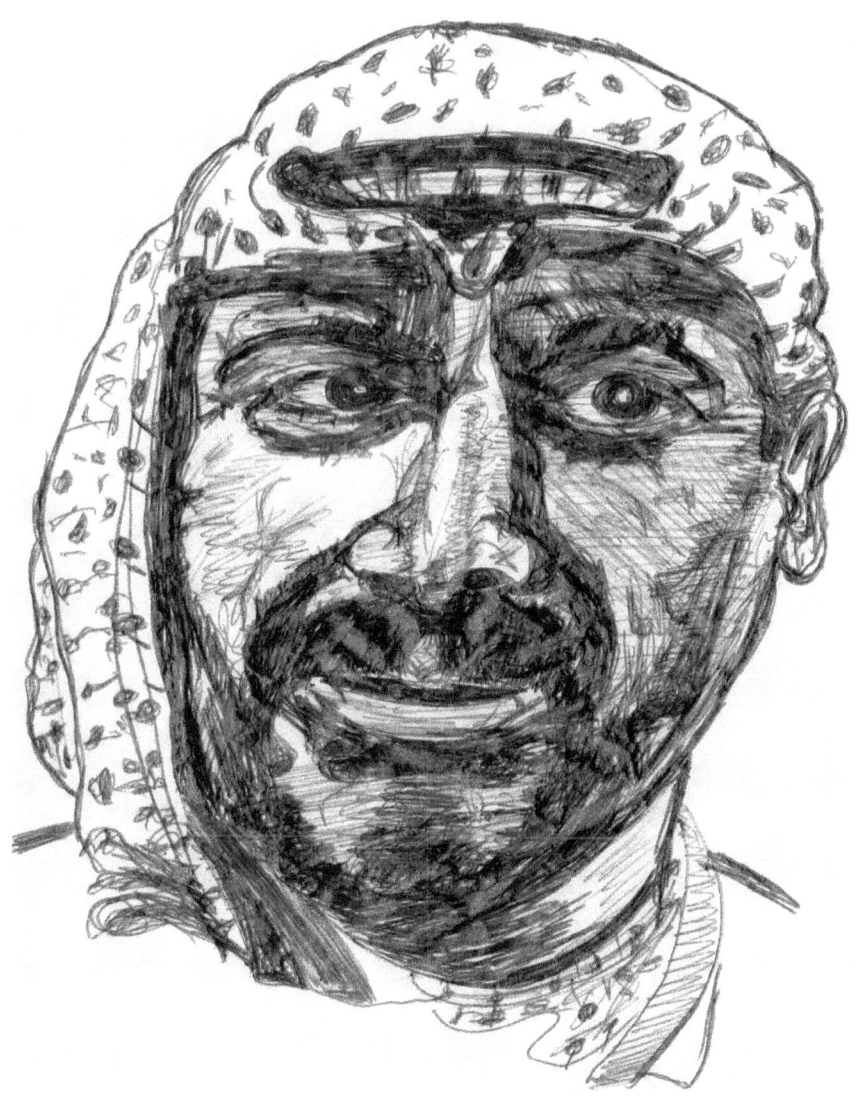

YASHA ARAFAT: Revolutionary figure and
Chairman of the Palestine Liberation Organisation.

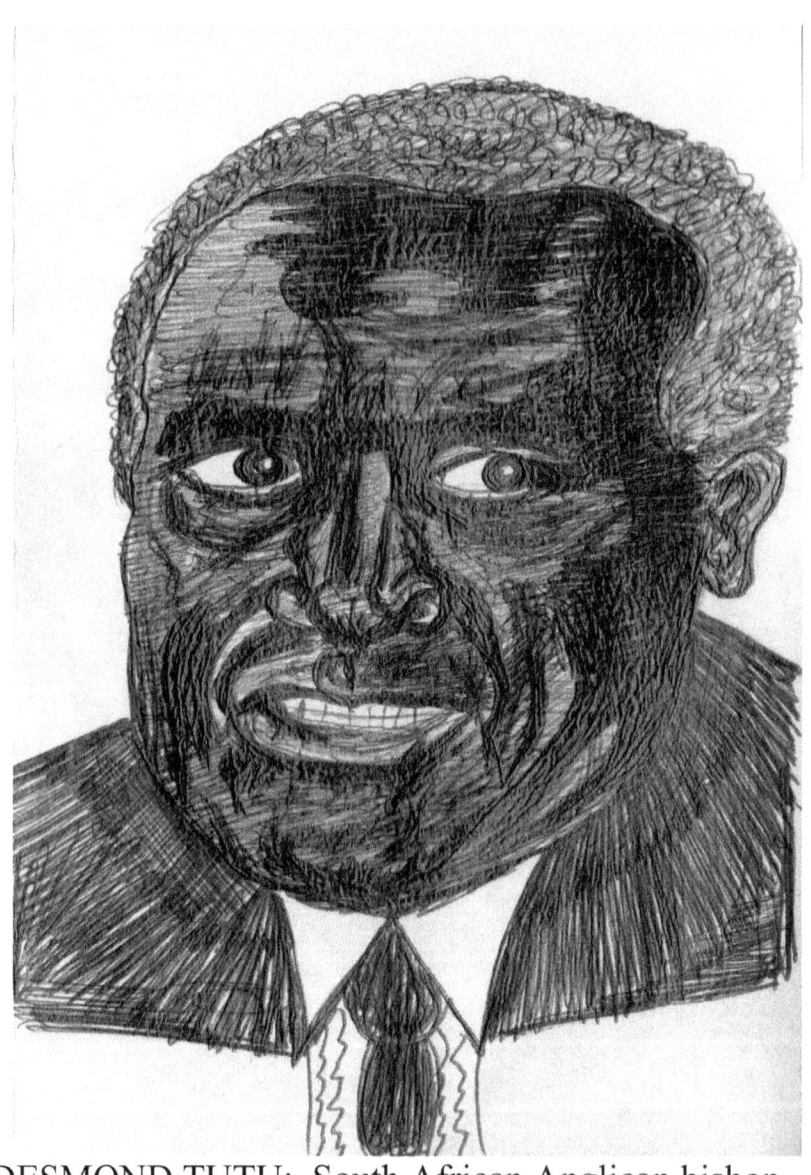

DESMOND TUTU: South African Anglican bishop, anti-apartheid activist and general champion of the oppressed and ill. The first black Archbishop of Cape Town. Nobel Peace Prize 1984.

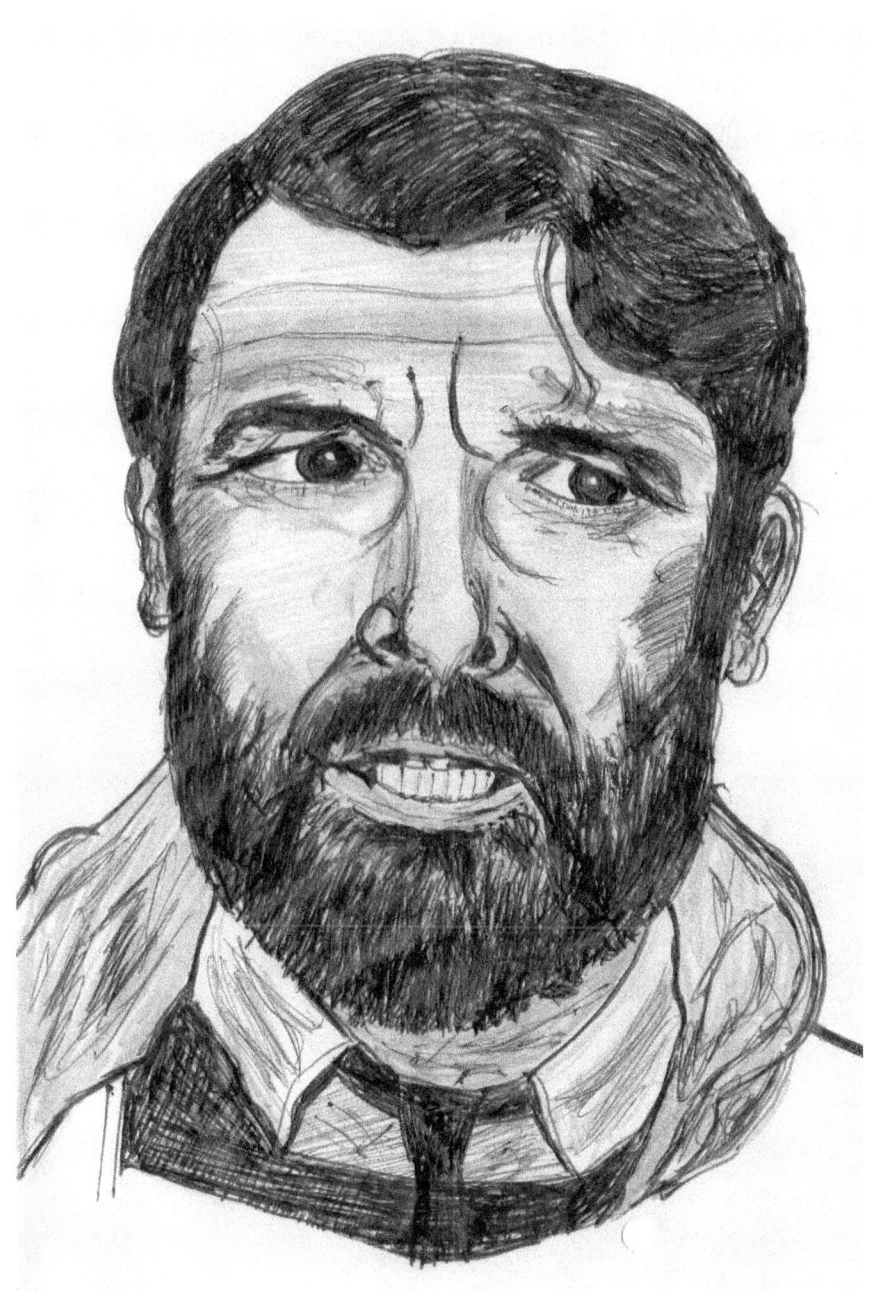

TERRY WAITE: Church of England envoy who travelled to Lebanon to secure the release of hostages, being held captive himself between 1987 and 1991. His faith never deserted him and he is now President and patron of several charities.

THE UNIDENTIFIED

Some figures are unidentified. If anyone recognises them, please tell me through my website www.robincalvert.co.uk and I will update the file.

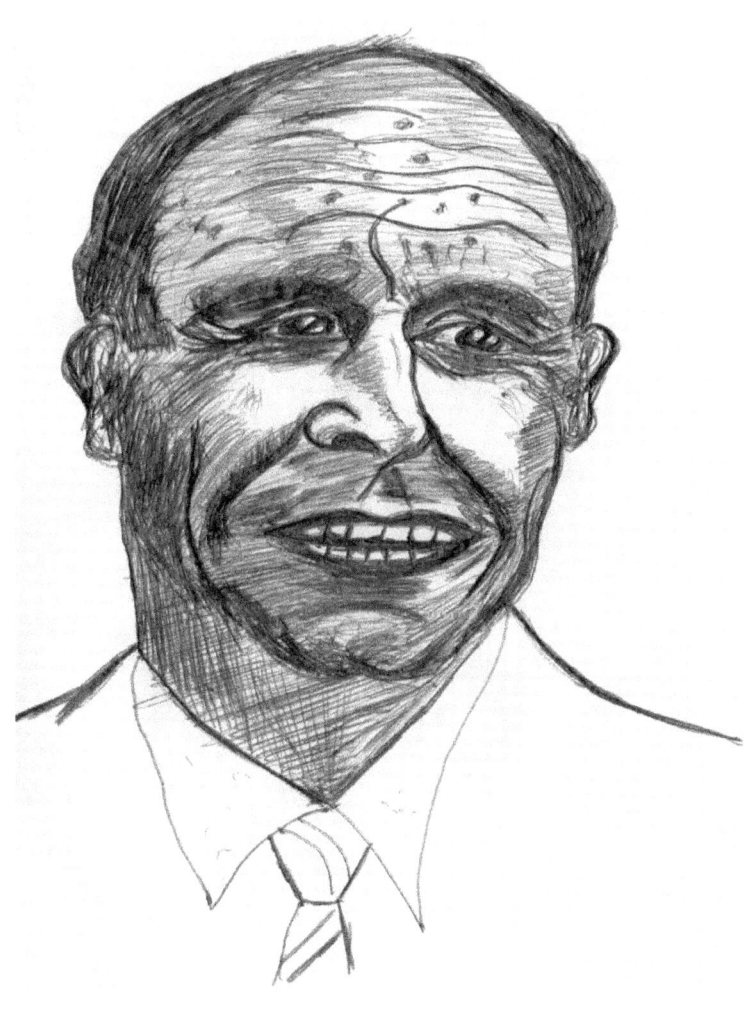

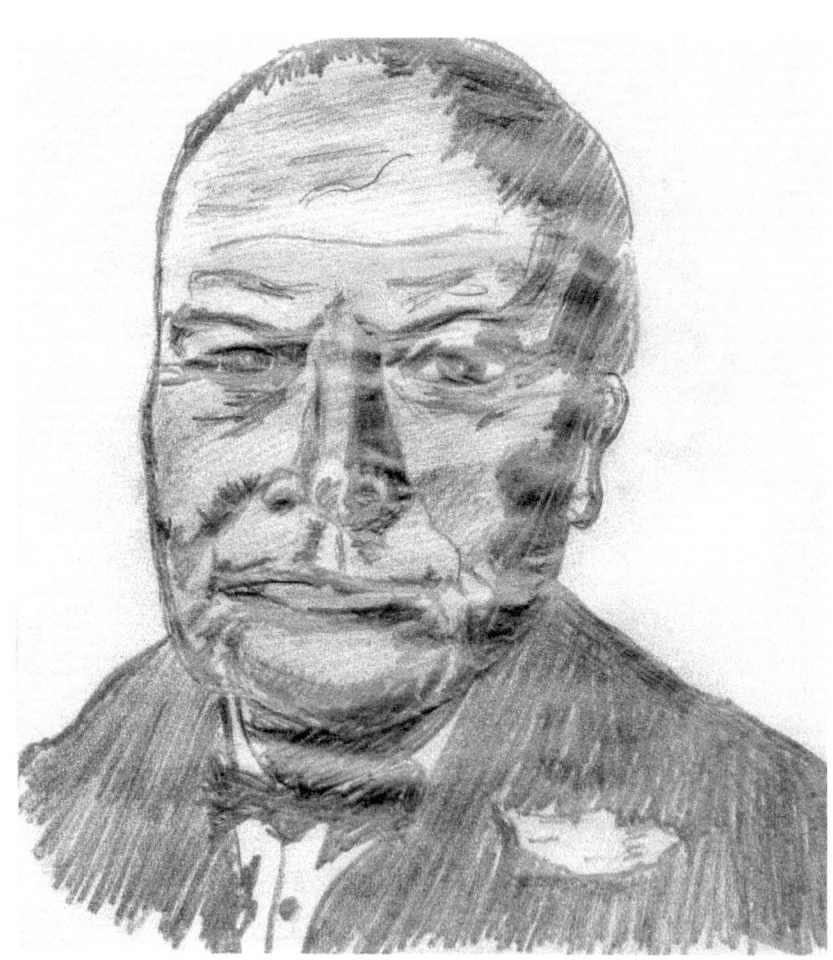

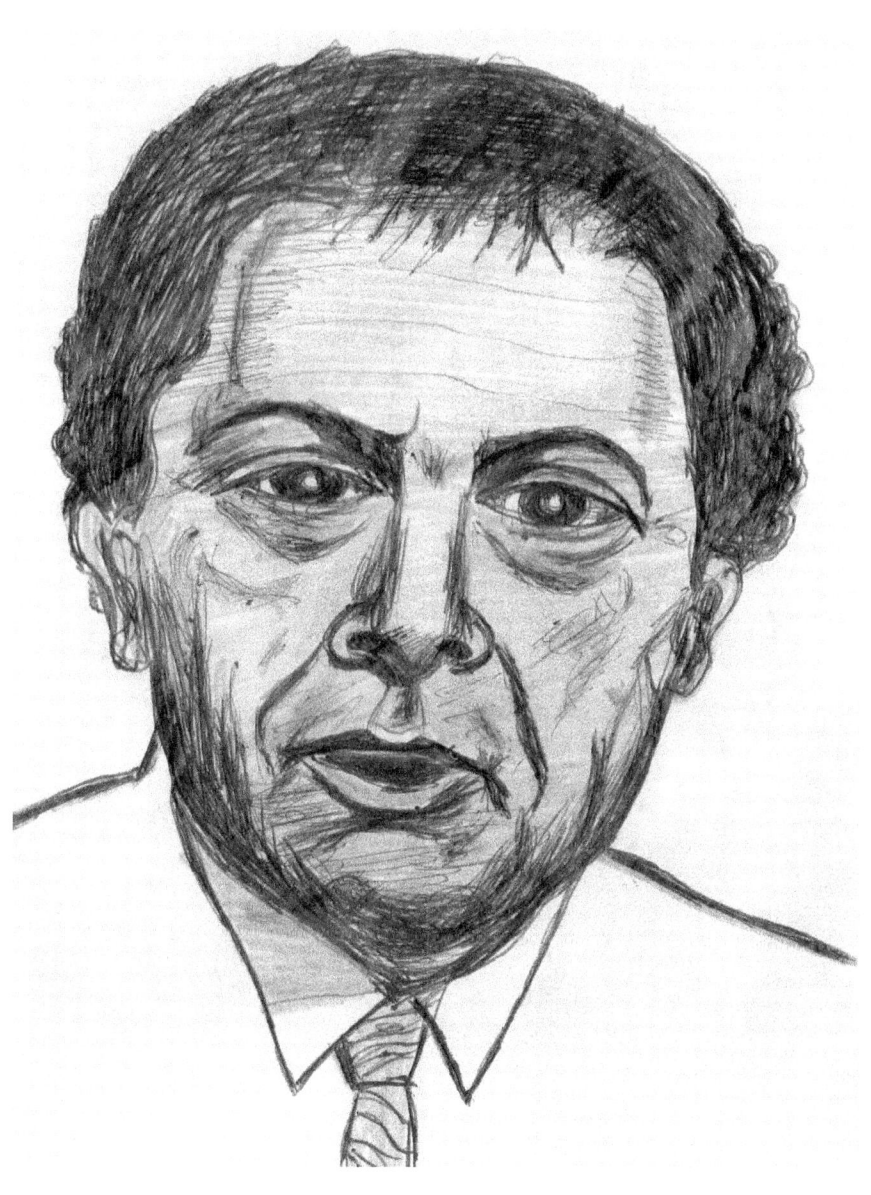

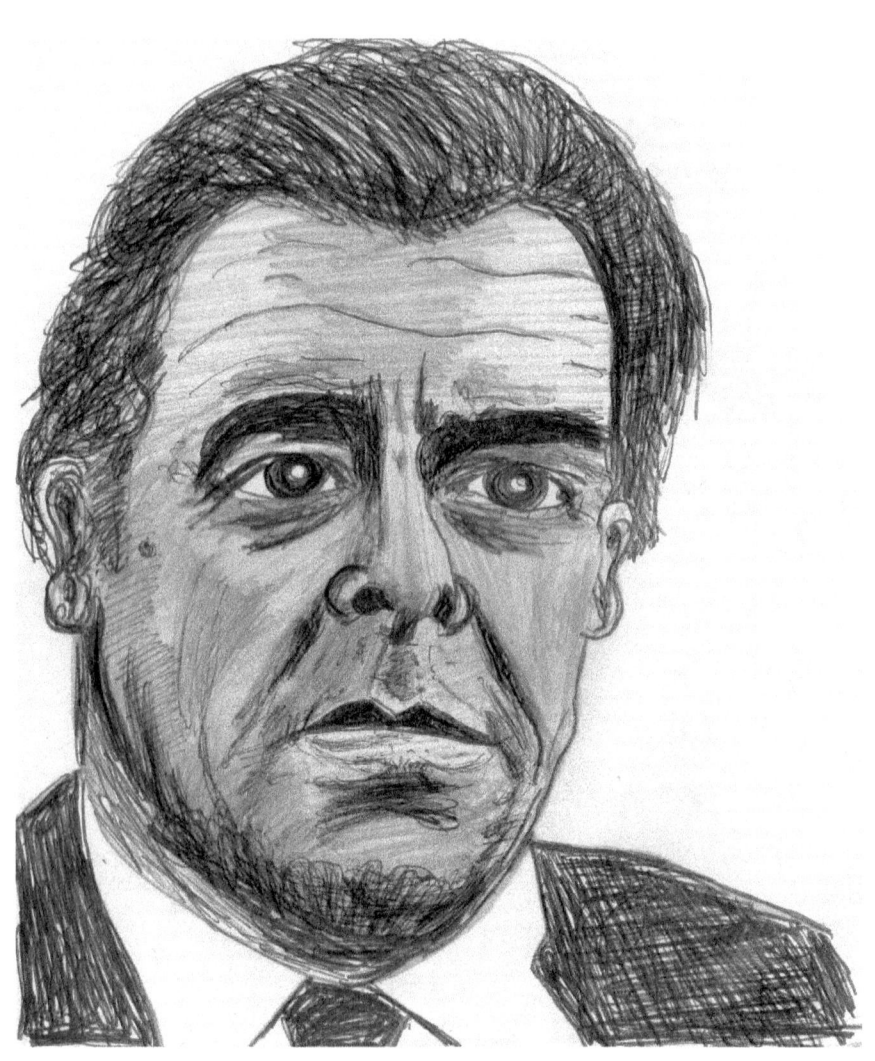

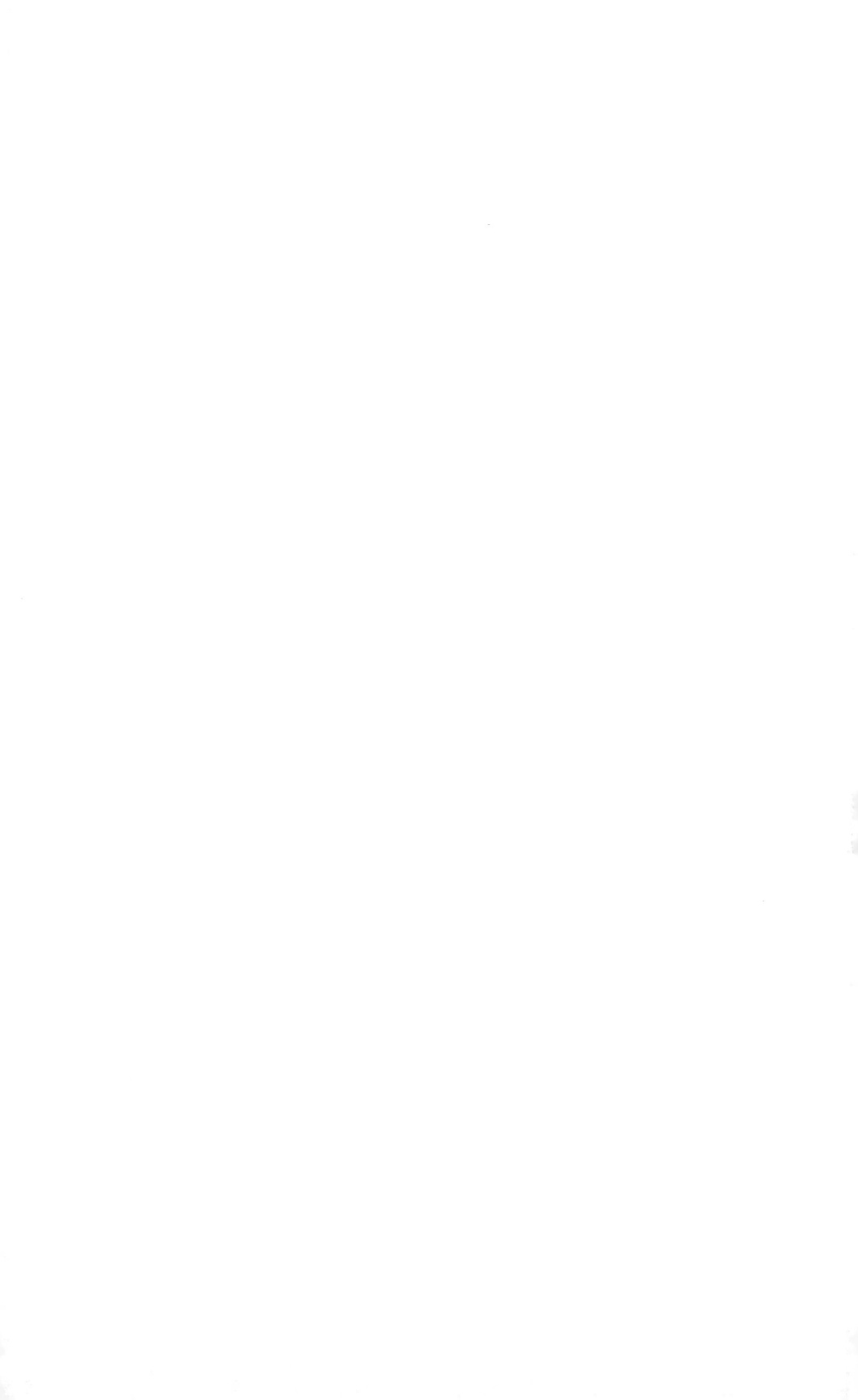

www.ingramcontent.com/pod-product-compliance
Lightning Source LLC
Chambersburg PA
CBHW071827170526
45167CB00003B/1457